The Greeks
in Asia

John Boardman

The Greeks
in Asia

208 illustrations, 50 in color

 Thames & Hudson

For JULIA

1 Indian gold finial inscribed ΘEA or 'goddess'. See PL. XXXVI.

The Greeks in Asia © 2015 Thames & Hudson Ltd, London

First published in 2015 in hardcover in the United States of America by
Thames & Hudson Inc., 500 Fifth Avenue, New York, New York 10110

thamesandhudsonusa.com

Library of Congress Catalog Card Number 2014952407

ISBN 978-0-500-25213-0

Printed in China by Toppan Leefung

Contents

Preface

In 1948 I met an elderly Greek man on the island of Naxos who said he had been with General Kitchener at Khartoum. As a boy he was helping his father sell lemonade to the British troops, undercutting the prices of the local Arab shopkeepers. The episode seemed typical of that Greek private enterprise and success far from home which was as apparent in antiquity as it is today, commercial rather than militant or imperial – consider Greek millionaire ship-owners. It may be that this quality was one imposed by the relative poverty of the homeland. When the first Greek-speakers approached the Mediterranean from the north they found themselves ushered into a peninsula whose south-ern extremity was far less well provided with arable or pastoral plains than most of the other countries bordering the Mediterranean; not at all like Italy or Spain. It inevitably led to a complex of independent and often competi-tive states rather than a united country, and this was apparent already under the Mycenaean Greeks in the Bronze Age, with their separate kingdoms and fortress capitals. Many Greeks took to the seas and looked to improve their fortunes elsewhere. The ancient world was a relatively small place: Indian cin-namon could be found in the Heraion of Samos in the 7th century BC, but had travelled hand-to-hand;[1] amber arrived from the Baltic. But the Greeks would soon learn the merits of distant travel for themselves.

They had come from the north and east originally.[2] Their presence in Greece, as what we call Mycenaeans, already provided opportunities to dem-onstrate their readiness to look both east and west, to Anatolia, to Cyprus, to Italy. Barely three centuries after the fall of the Mycenaean world in around 1200 BC their attention again inexorably turned away from the homeland. To the west they were partly looking for new homes, but were mainly acquisitive of the products and wealth of peoples of, by comparison, relatively modest cultural accomplishment and no threat.

The results were to mutual benefit: the Greeks grew richer and found some new homes; the westerners were introduced to a wider world for their produce, to a monetary economy, to literacy, and to an art that could express narrative explicitly, after some centuries of relative stagnation. They were not physically threatened. This is not quite 'colonization' in the modern sense of the word, but there are points of comparison and any sensible scholar or student is not misled by use of the word.

In the eastern Mediterranean the Greeks reintroduced themselves to the heirs of the great civilizations and empires of the Near East, and submitted to an orientalizing revolution in their arts, which was to lead inexorably to the classical revolution of the 5th century BC and the genesis of a mode of 'classical' civilization to which the whole Western world remains heir.

This book is about what happened when Greeks met easterners – Anatolians, Levantines, Persians, Asiatics, Indians; how they interacted and what effects there were on the arts and societies of distant lands being visited and even settled by these folk, whose own traditions had evolved through various forms of kingship, tyranny and empire, and whose arts had passed from the formal and abstract to a degree of observation of life and nature not attempted elsewhere in the then civilized world. And they were visiting settled civilizations far older than theirs, with their own strong traditions in life, government and the arts, of a yet more decisive and individual cultural stamp than the Greek. As elsewhere in the world, these interfaces between cultures present a fascinating study of how human societies evolve, and how progress is as at least as often the product of interaction as it is locally generated.[3] So this is not just a study of peoples and arts of non-Greeks who had been exposed to Greek culture at various levels, but more a study of the Greeks, 'the Greek' and the more broadly 'classical' in Asia, including material that can only be explained by acquaintance with Greek culture but not always involving the immediate presence of Greeks. And one result is a certain discontinuity of subject and date between some chapters (especially the non-Greeks of Chapters 3 and 7) in the attempt to keep like with like. 'The Roman' is also a problem since the Roman Empire spread east to as far as Mesopotamia and (much) later dealt directly with southern India. I have therefore to address the problem of 'Greek or Roman' arts and, without, I hope, demoting the Roman, stress the Greek character of so much in Roman Asia and especially at Alexandria in Egypt, which were the main sources of the classicism that passed east.

My treatment of the subject is not exhaustive, since there are several histories of the period and subject available, as well as thorough bibliographies and lists of sources. It tends to favour the primary evidence – physical, archaeological, artistic and literary, too often scorned by latter-day scholars – since this is often less easily found by the reader and has long been my main interest. Here too I am much dependent on the resources of a good library and the information supplied by colleagues.

The Greeks were not empire-builders, and for the most part the Asian cultures they met were far better organized to control great tracts of land, to aspire to ambitious conquest and to influence and eventually absorb other peoples. The Greeks had no such vision, and spent much of their time trying to foil each other. But they had other qualities which could be valued anywhere, as they had been in the west: they were adept at trade, they could be good accountants and organizers for others, they were highly literate, they spread a monetary economy for Eurasia, their religion was not too demanding and easily adapted to that of others, and their art developed a form of narrative that was to be dominant for centuries to come. Their poets and philosophers were widely respected outside their homeland. They are an odd phenomenon in world history, and through their travels they came to leave a very distinctive imprint on the lives and arts of many distant peoples, and over centuries, some to the present day.

My interest in the subject was generated at an early date by preoccupation with evidence for Greeks visiting the eastern shores of the Mediterranean, in Syria, as pirate-traders, in the 9th/8th century BC, as demonstrated by the type of Greek pottery they carried and which was locally copied. This revealed them to be from the island of Euboea, which was, we know, also the source of those Greeks who were starting to explore the western Mediterranean coasts, North Africa, Italy and Sicily. Their closest rivals were the Phoenicians, who were more ambitious, less versatile. All this led me to a more general study of Greeks overseas (the title for a book in 1964, much revised since, to 1999) in the earlier period. My enthusiasm was expanded as a result of travel, to Persia, Afghanistan, India and East Asia, of involvement in the *Crossroads of Asia* exhibition in Cambridge in 1992, and of a deliberate study for lectures on the diffusion of classical art in antiquity (*DCAA*; a book title for 1994), as well as a better acquaintance with the plentiful literature that has been devoted to those areas. New finds have generated new observations, to the point at which an assessment of results seemed desirable (as much for the writer as for any interested reader).

The Greeks' view of the Phoenicians is not easy to fathom. They do not become obvious rivals until a much later date and they seem to have moved west through the Mediterranean with a dividing line between their interests drawn by simple geography and the obvious routes rather than mutual antagonism – across the Adriatic into Italy for the Greeks, along the North African coast for the Phoenicians. Phoenician works appear in western Greek sites, though the North Syrian outweigh them in the beginning. And the early Phoenician sites in the west, even Carthage, are not without clear traces of Greek goods and probable presence, and as early as any Phoenician.⁴

In my book on the diffusion of Greek art (*DCAA*) the reader will find a more fully documented account of much of this subject, more art and archaeology, less history. I have obviously depended much on the published work of others, which it is becoming increasingly difficult to command, despite Internet sources.⁵ It is in the nature of the lands covered in this book and their exploration in the last two centuries, that much material of relevance has not been scientifically excavated and may be known only once it reaches the market. A minority of scholars would regard such material as untouchable, but it would be foolish, indeed unscholarly and smacking of censorship, to ignore it. Most forgeries are obvious, and there are major classes of material which are vital to our subject – such as coins – which simply cannot and should not be ignored. So I have not ignored them.

The Land

History starts in geography, and climate, but in the two-and-a-half thousand years since my narrative begins climate has not changed enough to need taking into account, although the activity of man – through cultivation and irrigation – may have affected local surroundings. In our area there are some serious mountain ranges but with passes, and generally speaking there are few places where passage could not somehow be effected. The Achaemenid Persians proved this by building a road network from the Aegean Sea to India and Central Asia[6] – not the least of their major contributions to the history of man and a project inconceivable for any Greek.

Our 'Greece' starts partly in Asia, on the west coast of Asia Minor (its Roman name; otherwise Anatolia, now Turkey). The west coast, as also the south and the offshore island Cyprus, resembles Greece, rugged with valleys, but fertile. Asia Minor is a high plateau, also rugged in the north and especially the northeast where the coast turns along the borders of the Black Sea, with a fertile enclave in modern Georgia, leading to the mountainous Caucasus to the north, and east to the Caspian Sea. South, the east coast of the Mediterranean, on to Egypt, is also fertile, giving way soon to desert. To the east lay the fertile valleys of the Tigris and Euphrates (Mesopotamia, 'between the rivers'), which emerge on to the Persian Gulf. Persia beyond is a sweep of mountain ranges with some fertile plains, then desert, ending in a plateau before what we call Central Asia. The mountain ridges run on through modern Afghanistan (the Hindu Kush), north Pakistan and ultimately Tibet.

The plains of Central Asia are crossed by two rivers – the Oxus (Amu Darya) running into the now dessicated Aral Sea, but once probably into the Caspian Sea, and the Syr Darya; and between lie massive plains, part desert but often fertile though lacking other natural definition than the rivers. But these river plains proved the bases for major towns, including some of the largest in antiquity. Otherwise these lands were more naturally occupied by nomad peoples. North of India and the high Tibetan plateau we are in an area where rise of many of the greatest rivers of Asia, the Indus, the Ganges, the Mekong, along with the sources of the great Chinese rivers, the Yangtse and Yellow, and not far off the 'Silk Roads' going east to China – the 'roads' in our period being simply a succession of staging posts, from the Mediterranean to the China Seas, where goods were handed on, and only incidentally on transcontinental highways (an Achaemenid Persian speciality).[7] And north there are more mountains (Tienshan) with routes to their north, through Siberia to China. The northern nomad lands are defined north–south, by the Urals running north of the Caspian, then the Irtysh and Yenisei (Minussinsk) river valleys, then Lake Baikal and Mongolia. Overall the climate varies from the tropical to a land of permafrost, the terrain from sheer desert to impenetrable forest.

Personal acquaintance with areas studied counts for a lot. I have not seen as much of Asia Minor and the Black Sea coast as I might wish, but have travelled most of the coastline, Georgia, and, in the Levant, parts of the coast from Al Mina to Petra. Iraq is unknown to me but Persia quite well travelled (1985, 2011), as also north Pakistan and Afghanistan (1978), with a trip beyond the Oxus (from Tashkent west, 2011), and east of Kashgar past the Taklamakan desert and on to China and the coast (1989). Even a fleeting visit helps to fix the history and geography. I am a great admirer of the historian Arnold Toynbee (whom I accompanied on a tour round Attica in 1949), who made a point of knowing the land as well as the literature, not always a merit of today's historians.[8] His view was that 'Human beings and human societies cannot be understood apart from their environment, and their geographical environment cannot be apprehended at second hand'.

I have declared that this is not designed to be a comprehensive account of the subject – that would take a lifetime and several volumes. I have tried to indicate and document its range and appeal, sparing the detail in areas well covered by others, notably the strictly 'historical', and paying more attention to the archaeological/art-historical aspects, since these have always been my primary interest; they are not easily assessed, and they are plentiful and multiplying year by year. My title is 'The Greeks' – but it includes much which must be Greek in inspiration although not necessarily from the hands of Greek-speakers. And I would add only one general observation. The Greeks were not empire-builders, but their culture contributed to the imperial history of Rome and to more than one empire to the east. The columns of their Temple of Artemis at Ephesus could match those of Persepolis (themselves Greek-inspired). They made a major intellectual and artistic contribution, directly, and indirectly by the example set by travellers and migrants, to much of that great geographical band of urban civilizations that stretched from China to Peru, which I attempted to define in my *World of Ancient Art* (2006), a feat that might excuse their many faults. Certainly, their art 'had something of the character of a virus in antiquity'.[9]

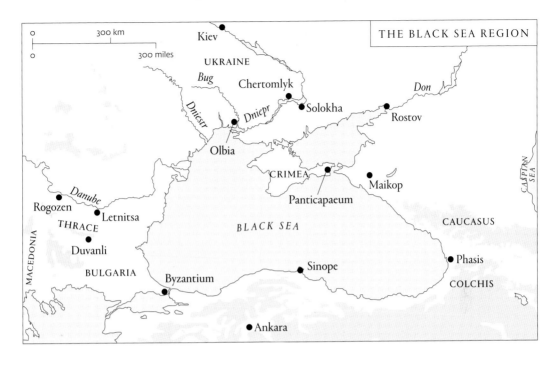

THE BLACK SEA REGION

Kiev

UKRAINE

Bug

Chertomlyk

Dniestr

Dniepr

Solokha

Don

Rostov

Olbia

CRIMEA

Panticapaeum

Maikop

CASPIAN SEA

Danube

Rogozen

Letnitsa

THRACE

Duvanli

MACEDONIA

BULGARIA

Byzantium

BLACK SEA

Sinope

CAUCASUS

Phasis

COLCHIS

Ankara

300 km

300 miles

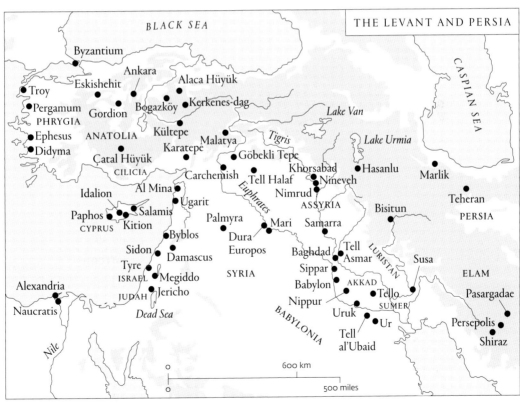

THE LEVANT AND PERSIA

BLACK SEA

Byzantium

Ankara

Eskishehit

Alaca Hüyük

Troy

Kerkenes-dag

Pergamum

Gordion

Bogazköy

PHRYGIA

Lake Van

Ephesus

ANATOLIA

Kültepe

Tigris

Lake Urmia

Didyma

Malatya

CASPIAN SEA

Çatal Hüyük

Karatepe

Göbekli Tepe

CILICIA

Khorsabad

Hasanlu

Carchemish

Tell Halaf

Nineveh

Marlik

Al Mina

Nimrud

Idalion

Ugarit

ASSYRIA

Teheran

Paphos

Salamis

Palmyra

Mari

Samarra

Bisitun

CYPRUS

Kition

Dura

Baghdad

PERSIA

Byblos

Europos

Tell

Sidon

Damascus

SYRIA

Asmar

Susa

Tyre

Sippar

LURISTAN

ELAM

ISRAEL

Megiddo

Babylon

AKKAD

Alexandria

JUDAH

Jericho

Nippur

Tello

Pasargadae

SUMER

Naucratis

Dead Sea

BABYLONIA

Uruk

Ur

Persepolis

Nile

Tell
al'Ubaid

Shiraz

600 km

500 miles

13

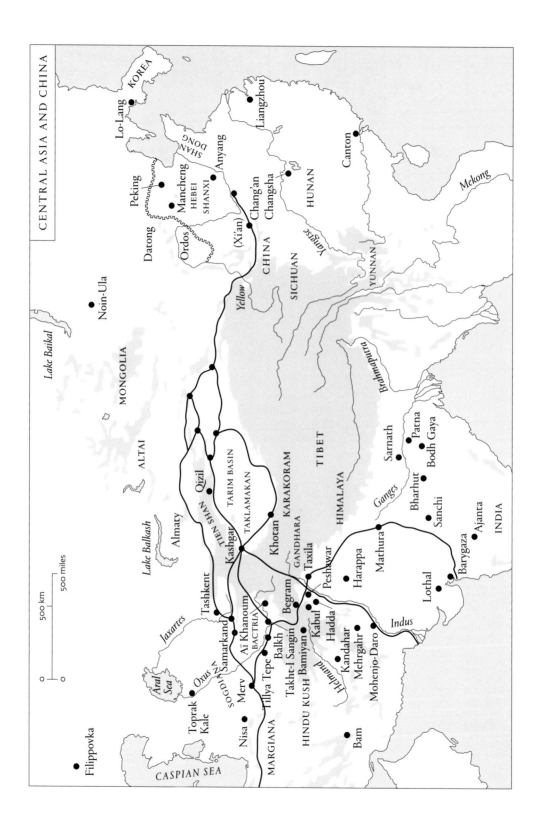

KOREA
Lo-Lang
Liangzhou
Anyang
SHAN DONG
Canton
Peking
Mancheng
HEBEI
SHANXI
Datong
Chang'an
Changsha
Ordos
(Xi'an)
CHINA
HUNAN
Yellow
SICHUAN
Yangtze
YUNNAN
Noin-Ula
MONGOLIA
Lake Baikal
Brahmaputra
ALTAI
Parna
Sarnath
Bodh Gaya
TIBET
Qizil
TARIM BASIN
Ganges
Bharhut
TIEN SHAN
TAKLAMAKAN
KARAKORAM
Sanchi
Almaty
Khotan
HIMALAYA
Ajanta
Lake Balkash
GANDHARA
INDIA
Kashgar
Taxila
Mathura
Barygaza
Tashkent
Peshawar
Harappa
Jaxartes
Begram
Lothal
SOGDIANA
Aï Khanoum
Kabul
Samarkand
BACTRIA
Hadda
Indus
Oxus
Balkh
Merv
Tillya Tepe
Takht-I Sangin
Kandahar
Aral
Sea
Bamiyan
Mehrgarh
Nisa
HINDU KUSH
Mohenjo-Daro
Toprak
Kale
MARGIANA
Helmand
Bam
Filippovka
CASPIAN SEA

500 km
500 miles

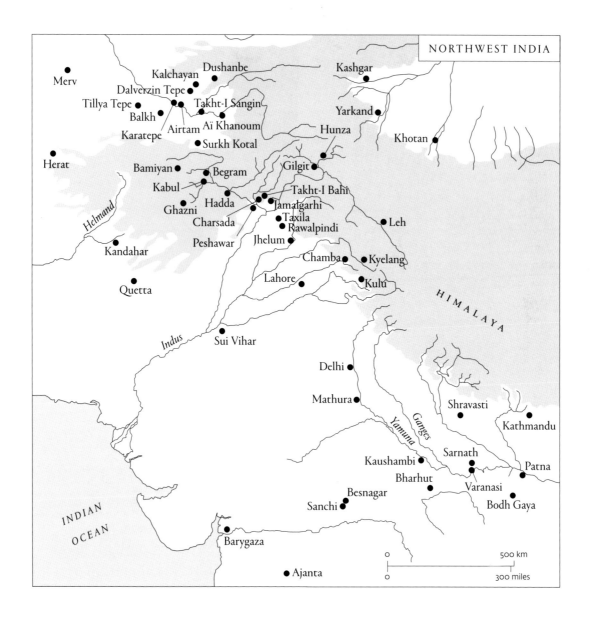

Merv

Kalchayan
Dushanbe
Dalverzin Tepe
Tillya Tepe
Takht-I Sangin
Balkh
Airtam
Karatepe
Aï Khanoum
Surkh Kotal

Kashgar

Yarkand

Hunza

Khotan

Herat

Bamiyan
Begram
Gilgit
Kabul
Takht-I Bahi
Ghazni
Hadda
Jamalgarhi
Charsada
Taxila
Peshawar
Jhelum
Rawalpindi
Leh

Kandahar

Chamba
Kyelang
Lahore
Kulu

Quetta

HIMALAYA

Indus

Sui Vihar

Delhi

Mathura

Shravasti

Kathmandu

Yamuna
Ganges

Kaushambi
Sarnath
Bharhut
Varanasi
Patna

Besnagar
Bodh Gaya

Sanchi

INDIAN
OCEAN

Barygaza

500 km

300 miles

Ajanta

15

CHAPTER 1
Greece and the east: beginnings

Eastern origins

The Greeks came from the east.[10] Their language belongs to the group known as Indo-European, whose original home was probably somewhere in Central Asia, to account for terms that seem to betray an appropriate shared way of life and for the links with languages of the Indian subcontinent. They entered Greece from the north, more probably from the upper Balkans and Black Sea area than from across the Bosporos 'bridge' from Anatolia. They found a country peopled by folk who boasted a strong Neolithic/Early Bronze Age tradition, which also had clear links with the east, probably most directly across the Aegean Sea. And to the south, on the island of Crete, there flourished the remarkable 'Minoan' civilization, indebted both to the east and Egypt, its people probably at first from Anatolia – not Greek. Of all the peninsulas dropping into the Mediterranean from the north the Balkan/Greek was the least promising agriculturally, relatively small (compare Italy, Spain), and it obliged the inhabitants of its southern extremity ('Greece'), if they had ambitions, to look overseas for places to settle or trade, while as a 'homeland' the geography was so diverse and divided that 'Mycenaen Greece' barely became a nation, rather than a consortium of independent kingdoms, and never again afterwards except at the dictate of Macedon or Rome. Whatever the character of the Greeks' genes, their new home was their greatest challenge, and the way they met that challenge determined much of the history of the western civilized world thereafter, and no little of the eastern.

In the Bronze Age the Greeks established kingdoms, from south of Mount Olympos, which was the natural northern boundary of their land and thus deemed to be the home of their gods, who are commonly so located (compare Valhalla), to the southern tip of the Peloponnese. They built castles (like Mycenae, Tiryns) and they crossed the Aegean. The presence of Greeks settled on that coast is attested archaeologically and from Hittite texts of about 1300 BC referring to Ahhiyawa (Achaea, the Greek name for Greece) and the Greek city at Millawanda (Miletus). There are even texts which some scholars relate to a conflict at Troy.

The Greeks went on as far as Cyprus, where we recognize them also for their language, because they had learned from the Minoans of Crete how to write – Linear B, the script deciphered in 1952 by Michael Ventris, whom I was lucky to count as a friend. They took over the Minoan world by around 1350 BC, but were themselves displaced less than two centuries later by other Greeks from the north, traditionally the 'Dorians', in circumstances that involved something more than force of arms (famine, disease?), and which effectively destroyed all the sophistication of the Mycenaean/Minoan world. It reduced Greece to a land of farmers and pastoralists, not knights, its writing forgotten. Behind the Greeks, north of Olympos, other people of related origin and language, but one not intelligible to the Greeks, occupied the upper part of the Greek peninsula and lower Balkans – Macedonians and Thracians, the latter with closer links to Anatolia. Thus it was until the 9th century BC, when some Greeks began to look east again, even beyond Cyprus, where 'Cypriot-Greeks' had devised a new syllabic script for the Greek language by around 1000 BC, strictly for local use. One result of the move beyond Cyprus was to be the creation of a new system of writing, alphabetic, also for the homeland Greeks, based on the Syrian Aramaic alphabet (itself adapted from the Phoenician), rather than the syllabary (b-a-b-a, rather than ba-ba), which continued long for the language in Cypriot-Greek. Alphabetic writing was to become the preferred mode in much of the civilized world.[11]

In the arts the new culture of Greece cast off the colourful naturalism of its Bronze Age past, and adopted Geometric styles of decoration, determined by the ruler and compass, inspired by the domestic arts of weaving and carpentry, an idiom of Europe but never there developed with the same precision and feeling for composition. Their towns were smaller but some were able to admit big, if relatively unsophisticated architecture, like the 'palaces' on the Euboean Straits (Lefkandi, Amarynthos). And by now all the Aegean islands and many new cities on the coast of Anatolia (Smyrna, Miletus, Ephesus) and offshore islands (Lesbos, Chios, Samos, Rhodes) were no less Greek than the homeland, so that the focus of the Greek world was as much the Aegean Sea as the southern Balkan peninsula.

Their exploration west was in the interests of finding trade or new homes, a form of 'colonizing', however the term is defined; and in parallel the Phoenicians were also exploring west but not provoking any serious competition with Greeks. In the west the Greeks met relatively unsophisticated peoples and, whatever the effect may have been for Greece, they undoubtedly transformed their lives, bringing them the profits of trade, soon a monetary economy, literacy, and a narrative art of great social potential, as I have already observed. Their fortunes to the east, their aims and achievements, could not be more different, yet the same Greeks are involved.

Greeks going east

It was the Euboeans, who have been mentioned for their precocious palace-building, who can first be identified as the Greeks with a presence on the east Mediterranean coast, just as it was to be the Euboeans who led Greeks in the 8th century to explore and settle in the western Mediterranean – and, indeed, in the northern Aegean beyond Mount Olympos. They are identified from their pottery, and since this criterion is of considerable importance for our subject in this early period it deserves some explanation.[12] Pottery serving the needs of eating, drinking, cooking and storage was also for the Greeks often a medium for decoration of varying degrees of sophistication, only approaching the luxurious in the later archaic and classical periods. But at all times the decoration betrays both origins within the Greek world and date, and in this the Euboean of the 9th/8th centuries BC was no exception.

At this time pottery was seldom if ever carried for its own sake, as it was later, by way of trade, for its attractive appearance if not as a luxury product. Instead it accompanied the folk who were best used to it, and so is a marker of their presence, especially when found in quantity. Isolated pieces could get anywhere, any time. It was pottery for the table, and especially for the almost ritual practices involved in drinking (in the symposium), that attracted the craftsman and on which he displayed his skills and betrayed his homeland preferences. An interesting criterion for us, apart from our ability to identify where in Greece the pottery was made, is the contrast with the east. Generally, the drinkers of the west and the Greek world drank watered wine – or at least wine is a principal marker of society at all levels. They drank in quantity, from large cups necessarily supplied with handles and feet; this had applied even in the Bronze Age. The easterners drank beer from large vessels via a straw or tube, or stronger drink in much smaller quantities, from small bowls and cups which are handleless and footless, balanced on the fingers; and they were more used to metal vessels, even of precious metal. In the Greek archaic period (6th century BC), when they were becoming more conscious of the east, the Greek potters copied eastern metal cup shapes, but necessarily made them larger, and with handles and feet, to create the most familiar of all decorated Greek pottery forms – the *kylix*.[13] The distinction is fundamental and long lived – Omar Khayyám's accompaniment to 'a book of verses underneath the bough, the jug of wine, a loaf of bread, and thou' was a small handleless bowl held easily in the palm of the hand, as shown on many an eastern painting, not a handled and footed goblet as in Europe. Centuries later the same contrast in drinking vessels is seen, from small handleless eastern cups, to big cups and saucers for tea-drinking.

So, while Greeks abroad might make use of local cooking and storage wares they were likely to carry their own drinking cups, as peculiar to their personal way of life as might have once been an Englishman's pipe in an environment of chewing tobacco or hubble-bubbles. And when we find a mass of Greek pottery from the 8th century BC at sites in Syria it is the cups that betray their presence, as well as, moreover, similarly shaped cups made locally, in Cyprus and perhaps Syria, to serve their special needs, and decorated in styles which compromise between the local and the Greek, the latter being dominant – the multiple brush pattern is Greek, the concentric circles within on an unpainted ground, Cypriot.

The high road to the east from the Mediterranean lay along the lower valley of the River Orontes in Syria, on past Antioch and Aleppo to Mesopotamia. The area had known Mycenaean Greeks in the Late Bronze Age, and was probably visited by them, to judge from finds near the coast (Sabouni) and farther inland (Alalakh). On the coast, at Al Mina, Greek pottery is found already in the 9th century BC but becomes prolific only from the second quarter of the 8th century, and remains so to after the Assyrian invasion (which went on to Cyprus), and to the end of the century. At that point the Euboean states (Chalcis and Eretria) fell out with each other, in the so-called 'Lelantine War', and the connexions with Al Mina become more with the East Greek world. The site maintains some Greek connection thereafter until Hellenistic times. In early days it is hard to judge its function – no doubt a busy entrepôt for trade with central Greece, taken over by East Greeks in the 7th century after the collapse of Euboean primacy there and in the homeland. That Greeks were the prime occupants is clear from the finds: overwhelmingly Greek pottery of the types and functions that local production could not meet – notably the Greek handled and footed drinking cup, and including cups of Greek type made in the east especially for Greek use – a prime indicator of Greek presence. That Greek pottery could be of interest *per se* to any easterner, for its Geometric decoration, is highly improbable. Only later did Greek potter-painters (notably the Athenian) begin to produce very elaborate and figure-decorated wares that might attract any customer.[14]

But there is other record of early Greek presence in the area, from eastern texts – as pirates, in sea battles and as coastal raiders who are dealt with by the Assyrians in 712 BC, with their leader Yamani ('the Greek') fleeing to Egypt. Their probable presence (i.e., much pottery) had spread also, up to Tarsus in Cilicia, which had ultimately to be dealt with by the Assyrians. There were Greek mercenaries too along the Levant coast in the 7th century. Just south of Tel Aviv, at Mesad Hashavyahu, what seems to be a Greek mercenary camp of the 7th century has been excavated, and another perhaps, at Tell Kabri inland.[15] By this time Greeks had been busy establishing 'colonies' for various purposes in Italy; in the east, however, they could not expect to be allowed any comparable independence of behaviour, since their neighbours were powerful heirs to long-established cultures of some sophistication. But they were tasting the east, and in depth, and in these centuries the arts and general culture of Greece take on an orientalizing flavour which will determine the future of Greek art. Soon Greek objects and, we can be sure, Greeks themselves became very familiar along the whole eastern coast of the Mediterranean.[16] For the easterners' attitude to the newcomers we are rather at a loss, apart from the Assyrian records' mention of their mainly hostile or disruptive activity. The Assyrians called them *Yavana*, a term with long currency and far to the east.[17]

This diffusion of Greeks and their influence brought them close to Near Eastern powers, in Syria and Assyria, but also to the Phoenicians, a seagoing power like the Greek, and a people with whom the Greeks would have much to do, although more in their western colonizing adventures than at home, since Greeks and Phoenicians were jointly or at least simultaneously exploring the west from the 9th century on, as in the Carthage area.[18] The Phoenicians operated from a few rich ports on the Levant coast (Byblos, Tyre, Sidon) rather than more extensive mainland territories, like the Syrians. They had learned an alphabetic script, which the Syrians then adapted for a language (Aramaic) which was to spread rapidly through the east and become the official language of the Persian Empire, and whose alphabet was adjusted by the Greeks during the 8th century BC to serve their own language.

The 'orientalizing revolution' in Greek art had started in the late 9th century – notably in Crete, which seems not represented among the Greeks who went east, and suggests that some easterners may have gone west too. Other early eastern finds, as in Euboea, show eastern goods from various sources arriving, probably in this case in Greek hands, but in Crete it seems more likely that craftsmen too were involved, to judge from the very idiosyncratic character of early archaic Cretan art,[19] not much shared by Greeks to the north, and with far more to do with Cyprus and Syria (and Urartu, beyond) than Phoenicia. Phoenician arts owed more to Egypt than Assyria, and some, notably the mass production of minor objects and scarab seals in 'faience' (glazed composition), and a few metal and perfume vases, were copied in Greek workshops (in Rhodes and Ionia to the north). But, for all the complexity of the following centuries of Phoenician ('Punic' in the west, at Carthage) and Greek (then Roman) relations in the west, Greek presence in the Phoenician homeland, apart from a few mercenaries, remained of somewhat less moment than their early presence farther north in Syria.

There are, however, other areas east of Greece, in Anatolia, whose seaboard had long been at least partially Greek, where intercourse with the foreigner was of growing importance, and where, soon, a new eastern power would call for all the Greeks' skills in diplomacy and negotiation, ultimately to be resolved on the battlefield. The kingdom of Lydia, its capital at Sardis, was the closest to the Greek coastal cities, and in many respects dominated them without occupying them, since Lydians were not seagoers and may for long have been relatively indifferent to their maritime neighbours. The relationship can be illustrated by two case studies – the coastal cities of Smyrna and Ephesus.

Lydia's capital was at Sardis, not too distant from the sea, but the Lydians seem at first to have had little interest in the coast or in the opportunities it might offer for yet more sources of wealth – Sardis was built on a river (Pactolus) in which gold dust flowed. However, the Greek cities on the coast were busy places. They looked inland to areas which they readily embraced into Greek myth-history – a Greek characteristic that I shall have to address at the end of this book but which will often recur. So, in the coastal mountains they could identify or find inspiration for Greek heroines turned to stone (Niobe), and see images of gods and kings in what were in fact old Hititte reliefs.[20] Positive hostility towards the Greeks on the part of the Lydians, and no doubt provoked by the Greeks, appears by the end of the 7th century. This was the time, oddly enough, when Greeks of the area were inventing coinage (struck metal) with Lydian gold and some apparently Lydian devices, in effect creating a monetary economy for their neighbours and themselves, and ultimately for all the west, for all the world [2]. In this respect at least we can suspect an interest of the Lydians in their neighbours and their potential. Early Greek Smyrna (the site of Bayraklı) had been occupied from the late Bronze Age on [3]. It lay beside a

2 Gold coin from Halicarnassus. The device is a stag, inscribed in Greek 'I am the sign [*sema*] of Phanes'. Early 6th cent. BC.

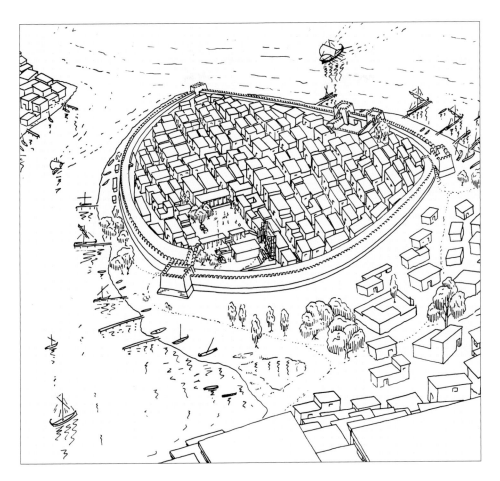

3 Reconstruction of the city of Old Smyrna (Bayraklı). 6th cent. BC.

good harbour, to the north of Izmir, the modern city that recalls its name. It was excavated by British and Turkish archaeologists after World War II (the writer among them), who found good evidence both for the monumentality of many of its buildings, among the earliest of the true Greek Ionic style, and for its fall, documented in passing by ancient historians. The site is a low hill and one might expect the crown of the hill to be its acropolis, but at Smyrna it forms the top of a massive siege mound built by the Lydians so that they could take the city simply by walking over its walls – an eastern military strata-gem.[21] The site revived slowly in antiquity until it was replaced by Hellenistic Smyrna, a bastion of Greekness until 1922.

Farther south, at Ephesus, the Greeks had a different experience of the Lydians. In the mid-6th century Croesus, of fabled wealth, was on the Lydian throne and apparently friendly to the Greeks, if only intermittently. The Ephesians were building a new temple to their goddess Artemis, which was to be the biggest in the Ionic style for that period and for long afterwards, lavish with relief sculpture and presenting an aspect of a sea of tall columns with elaborated capitals and bases, and with inscriptions on the column bases which tell that Croesus himself contributed to the construction. I think there must be a strong suspicion that he was a major promoter and patron of the site, for all the Greekness of its architecture and sculpture. So the Lydians were by then decidedly friendly, even seeming to court the Greeks, with gifts also to the big Apollo sanctuary at Didyma (near Miletus), while Croesus was generous also to Greek sanctuaries in the homeland, sending rich offerings to Delphi. It has been suggested, with some conviction, that Lydian patronage of the Greek cities of Ionia was a deliberate instrument of policy and even an encouragement to them (notably at Miletus) to develop trade with Egypt through the foundation of Naucratis in the Nile delta at the end of the 7th century, and probably also to explore the Black Sea shores.[22] The Lydians were not seagoers, but Croesus had imperial aspirations, which were to lead to his downfall and the arrival of the Persians on the shores of the Aegean. So we have perhaps to view these 'east Greeks' as already to some degree 'oriental-ized', at least in their allegiances. Certainly, their Artemis of Ephesus seems as much an eastern goddess as a Greek one for her form and function, and from the beginning dedications to her have a strong eastern flavour and even pro-venience, from Central Asia,[23] while later, under the Persians, local Anatolian non-Greek gifts are directed to her.

Throughout this period growing Greek infiltration from along the coasts of Anatolia proceeded, in areas long before visited by them but now settled. Caria, home to Herodotus, was heavily hellenized. In Lycia (southwest Anatolia) a Greco-native kingdom developed embracing much Greek in its arts, blended with native styles which recall even the Hittite in some respects. And so on to the east, to Cilicia, where we pick up the story that started at Al Mina in the 8th century BC, when there is a substantial Greek presence also

at Tarsus. Part-Greek Cyprus lay offshore, and its Greekness is evident from
the names of many of its local kings in the 7th century, while Greek presence
and enterprise were already permeating much of the seas and coasts of this
corner of the Mediterranean.

Turning far north, into the Black Sea, we find that Greeks had been
approaching the area already with, again, Euboean foundations along the
north coast of the Aegean, and an Ionian interest in the sea's east coast,
in modern Georgia, ancient Colchis, which offered a route straight on to
the Caspian Sea.[24] In the 7th century they were exploring the western and
northern coasts of the Black Sea, and planting colonies, as neighbours to the
Scythians of the south Russian plains. This was their first really close contact
with the Asian peoples of the steppes. The Scythians were a branch of the
Asian nomads of whom we shall hear much more (as the 'Saka'), but they
had settled north of the Black Sea, without too much adjusting of their non-
sedentary culture. The Greeks appreciated their wealth, and their corn. Greek
arts were very unlike the Scythian, but the eastern people took to them and
Greeks were soon busy making precious objects for the Scythians, adjusting
their style often to Scythian taste. Thus, on the gold mirror from Kelermes
[4],[25] we see a local myth – the Arimasps fighting the griffins who guarded Asian
gold – and tucked into the base of one of the segments, a small animal figure
executed wholly in the Scythian 'Animal Style', quite non-Greek. Moreover,
on another mirror from the same find is a button bearing a 'Rolltier' of a
type most familiar in steppe art.[26] Later, we find that the Persians faced the
Scythians in the north, but turned back, while the Greeks continued to help
furnish grand Scythian tombs, which display a blend of the steppe style of
the nomads with a degree of monumentality. This is a very special corner
of Greek intrusion into Asia, strongly localized and distinctive – also distinct from their other experiences of western Asia farther south, which we
have considered. It is worth dwelling on as a good example of Greek adapta-
tion to the interests of Asians.[27] Conspicuous are the examples of studies
of Scythians at ease, rendered in a purely Greek classical idiom: seated at a
feast [PL. II], even suffering dentistry – subjects quite foreign to steppe art.[28]
Gold quiver covers are decorated with Greek heroic, even Homeric scenes,

4 Electrum-plated silver mirror from Kelermes including a scene of the Arimasps attacking a griffin, a Goddess of Animals and a coiled creature in nomad style. (St Petersburg, Hermitage Museum. Diam. 17 cm)

as well as an important Greek innovation that was much taken up in Asia, a god or goddess shown with florals rather than legs below the waist, here with animal attachments and holding a decapitated human head [5],[29] exceptional later versions of which we shall find farther east. Beside these are many objects purely Greek in decorative style and subject, but of types current in

5 Gold plaque from Kul Oba.
A winged goddess with leonine
extremities holding the severed
head of a satyr (?). (St Petersburg,
Hermitage Museum)

6 Gold relief of a maenad holding a cup, wearing Greek over nomad dress, riding a lion,
from the Bliznitsa tumulus. (St Petersburg, Hermitage Museum. Drawing, author)

the northeast rather than the Greek homeland, like the pectoral and comb
[**PL. I**].[30] The god Dionysos, as ever, is not far away, but on a plaque showing
one of his maenads with a cup seated on a lion [**6**][31] we see that she has under
her Greek dress a thick-sleeved jacket of nomad type – well wrapped up, and
also to be recalled later in Asia [**PL. XXXI**].

Colchis (modern Georgia) has more in common with Greek practices in Anatolia, as one might expect, but there are many features and forms of local type but Greek style and subject (mainly animals) [7],[32] and here the Persians were to be in occupation also.

And finally, yet farther south again, in Egypt (not in Asia, so playing no part in this story) we have seen that Greek enterprise could have been triggered by Lydian interests. From the later 7th century on the east Greeks, and some mainlanders (from Aegina), had been allowed to establish themselves in a port of trade at Naucratis, as far up one of the arms of the Nile as big ships could go, and a promising trade with Egypt, carefully regulated by the Egyptians, would continue to flourish, through Egypt's 'Persian period' until the end of the 4th century BC when Egypt itself became 'Greek'/Macedonian and the city of Alexandria was founded. The placing of Naucratis leads me to wonder whether it was not to enable most easily the collection and export of salt, which was locally accessible and plentiful from the natron deposits close by, for pickling fish, a mainstay of the Mediterranean diet, also being at all periods a major attraction for trade and a necessity for life in growing populations.[33]

7 Gold plaque from a torque, featuring lions attacking bulls. From Vani, Georgia. (Tbilisi Museum. After *DCAA*)

CHAPTER 2
Greeks and Achaemenid Persia

The confrontation

A glance at a globe shows how Persia (modern Iran) lay at the crossroads of the Old World. It controlled the routes west–east, the only alternatives being north of the Caspian Sea in areas whose topography rather dictated that they were the territory of nomads rather than armies or city-businessmen, or by sea around Arabia, not to be much exploited by merchants or others until centuries AD. Between Persia and Anatolia lay Mesopotamia (Assyria/Babylonia) the home of the oldest sophisticated civilizations of western Asia; and southwest there was Egypt, but in relative decline by the 6th century BC.[34]

Prehistoric Persia had been the host to various important cultures, influential east and west, and most of them originally deriving from Central Asia rather than the west. The land is large, rugged and much is occupied by near-desert, but with areas of rich farmland and mineral resources. It has inevitably held a pivotal position in world politics (of whatever size the given 'world') from antiquity to the present day, when its culture (non-Arab, Islamic) and resources can still shake the confidence of self-styled 'world leaders'.

The Persians had entered their new homeland from Central Asia on the heels of the Medes, whose distinctive dress and cavalry manners they copied. The Greeks could often refer to the Persians as Medes, and the 'empire of the Medes and Persians' is a common rubric. The Persians were gentlemen, but they could also be ruthless. Herodotus, the Greek historian whom we shall discuss more fully later, characterized them as truth-telling and disciplined, only taken by luxury after they had conquered Lydian Croesus and seen his court in the mid-6th century BC. They exhibited perhaps a little less of the sheer cruelty displayed by many ancient peoples, including the Greeks.[35] Women knew their place; among the hundreds of sculptured figures decorating the palaces and buildings of Persepolis there is not one woman, but for a gift from Greece [**PL. VI**]. Women possibly enjoyed a better life (relatively) in Greece and Central Asia.[36] Persian religion was straightforward. A major deity was Ahura-Mazda, a version of the eastern sun god, and characteristic religious buildings are fire-temples, many of them quite modest buildings, centred on an ever-burning flame. Zoroastrianism was also somehow incorporated; this was the cult of the Asian prophet (Zarathustra to us), whose heritage survives still in parts of Persia and in India (the Parsees).[37]

By the middle of the 6th century the Persian royal family, known as 'Achaemenid' from their ancestor Achaemenes, was strongly established as a major power in the Near East, and looked to express this in buildings suitable to empire, and in an expansion of territory which would make for increased wealth and enable them to exercise what seemed to be their genius at regulating the lives and fortunes of foreigners – eventually to as far away as the borders of Greece, the shores of the Black Sea, deep into Asia and through Egypt. Their empire was divided into 'satrapies' with Persian governors (satraps), and each paid annual tribute to the king in Persia. Within each satrapy the Persian officers lived in a style that they had grown to enjoy in their homeland, even imitating Persian royal architecture, but they readily absorbed and exploited local customs. Generally, they seem not to have been much resented, but any revolts, whether generated by ambitious satraps or the ruled, were crushed.

The Persians knew how to run an empire peacefully, although they were ruthless with dissent. Their new subject Greeks in Anatolia seemed not too dissatisfied. Cyrus had started the expansion west – first Babylonia, then much farther off subduing Croesus in Lydia, where he met the Greeks. The native kingdoms of Anatolia (Lydia, Phrygia, Caria, Lycia) succumbed and lost much of their identity as a result. Royal roads were built across continents to knit the empire, and administration from Persia meant a busy exchange of letters, together with the eastern practice of sealing them. The Greeks were literate and numerate, quite ready to serve such new masters, as we shall see.

But Persian expansion was halted short of the Greek mainland. In the early 5th century Darius sent an army to subdue Greece, and while there were several Greek states (indeed, a majority) ready enough to serve or exploit a new master, the Athenians were not. At Marathon (490 BC) the Persians learnt that they were up against a 'free' people whose way of life and techniques of warfare were not easily overwhelmed by mere numbers, and that their rugged love of freedom could even at times outdo their readiness to seek profit. In 480 BC Darius' successor, Xerxes, sent another army, over two years, via north Greece. As the poet A.E. Housman put it, 'Their fighters drink the rivers up, their shafts benight the air. And he that stands will die for nought, and home there's no returning. The Spartans on the sea-wet rock sat down and combed their hair'. Although Xerxes swept past the Spartans at Thermopylae and took Athens, eventually his forces were sent back from the embattled waters of Salamis and the fields of Plataea, and the Persians decided that they might as well leave mainland Greece alone: a poor country anyway, troublesome, no real threat, not immediately accessible by land and easier to manage with Persian gold. So the Greeks reverted to fighting each other, inventing a fairly low-level democracy in Athens, where wealth could be flaunted readily only in the service of the state (financing the theatre or the navy), and flirting with Persian gold from the other side of the Aegean Sea when and as it suited them and the Persians. The Athenians kept up some pressure on Persia on the coast of Asia Minor, even defeating a Persian force at the battle of the Eurymedon (see below), but there was to be no further major confrontation and the Greeks came to contribute much to the culture of 'Greco-Persian' Asia Minor, with Lydia now out of the way, as we shall see. The archaeology and the art of the area (plus Herodotus) are a good corrective to the rather triumphalist attitudes of most Greek writers. The repulse of the Persians was indeed heroic, but rather a sideshow for world history until a non-Greek thought to avenge it.

Greeks in the Persian Empire

Herodotus, 'the Father of History', was born in Halicarnassus, towards the south of the west Anatolian coastline. He came from a family with literary pretensions, with names suggesting that he was of mixed Greek and Carian blood. He was born around the 480s BC, a vassal of the Persian Empire, although he seems to have stayed little at home, living for periods in Samos, Athens and south Italy, but also travelling extensively throughout the Persian Empire. He must have known Aramaic, the lingua franca of the empire, and when he says that all Persian names end in *s*, this applies only to Aramaic and Greek, not Old Persian (probably little spoken outside the homeland). He wrote his *History* so that 'the great and wonderful actions of the Greeks and the Barbarians should not lose their due meed of glory, and withal to put on record what were their grounds of feud'. So he explores the background – largely mythical – to Greco-oriental relations, and significantly begins with Croesus, as have we, going on both to describe the 'Persian Wars' in Greece, and the Persians, their empire and its neighbours. While writing what was in its way a panegyric to Greek arms he was no less critical of much Greek behaviour, and he was equally able to recognize the merit of many Persian customs. Otherwise he was a vigorous collector of anecdotes, but critical of them (for his day, remarkably so), and with a deep curiosity about the way the non-Greek peoples behaved. There are those who believe that he invented too much. I think we might, with hindsight, conclude that he sometimes believed too readily, but his reporting has proved most accurate, wherever we have other sources to check, and these range over archaeology, other Greek writers, and even a Chinese historian.[38] He often reports 'what others say' without admitting whether he believes them or not. Herodotus is not our only written source for Greeks in the east but he is a witness of inestimable value.

Another witness, Xenophon, actually served the Persians and gives us a fine insight on Persian manners. He was a young Athenian aristocrat born about 428/7 BC, and a familiar of Socrates. He left Athens in 401 and joined the army of the Persian prince, the younger Cyrus, who coveted the throne, and he gave an account (his *Anabasis*) of Cyrus' unsuccessful expedition against his brother Artaxerxes in Asia Minor. But he greatly admired the Persians and wrote an account (*Cyropaedia*) of the education of Cyrus the Elder, founder of the empire, treating him as a model hero. It is quite fictional but it reveals what Xenophon admired in Persian royalty, the sense of honour and discipline which we once associated with the public schoolboy serving his family and country ('Waterloo won on the playing fields of Eton'). In a way they stood at odds with Greek behaviour.

We have had reason already to look at Greeks and Lydians, and there is much more to tell of Greek fortunes in Anatolia under the Persians. The area was to continue to be the site for battles which we might regard as aftermaths of the Persian invasion, and often (we are told by Greeks) with some Greek success, as at Eurymedon, on the south coast, where, in about 467 BC, the Athenian general Kimon beat the Persians first at sea, then on land. But we can hardly regard this as more than a gesture, or doubt that, on foreign soil, it would have been unlikely that a Greek army could have dealt with an imperial Persian one.

Persian satrapies in Asia Minor seem to have encouraged even more infiltration of Greeks and Greek ways than had the kings of Lydia. Art, archaeology and the economic record tell the story. One product is a form of sub-archaic art which was practised while the Greek homeland was busy developing new 'Classical' styles, but which suited both the old Anatolian traditions and the new imperial arts of Persia, themselves in Greek terms 'sub-archaic' as we shall see.[39] Thus, metalwork closely reflects older Anatolian and Persian shapes and patterns, but it may be that the common use of figure and animal decoration as well as or instead of the traditional flutes, lobes and florals, had something to do with Greek preference for the figure-decorated. Animal-frieze decoration, often on small silver vessels and in a fine linear-incised style, lingers here longer than in the homeland and in a still broadly archaic style [8].[40] Here and there an animal form is rendered in a relaxed Greek manner without the formal eastern patterning.[41] Certainly, even some Greek floral inventions, ultimately derived from the east, returned to decorate eastern objects.[42]

Seal engraving is a sensitive art in this area, since the Persians were great bureaucrats, and letters flew throughout the empire along the new roads, in the form of clay impressed tablets each sealed with the sender's device – generally from a cylinder seal or, especially in the west, a stamp seal of Babylonian type ('pyramidal'). The latter seems notably current in Anatolia and several have been found bearing Lydian or Phrygian inscriptions (not Greek but in scripts derived from the Greek). The figure devices are mainly of the expected Persian imperial type – kings, gods and monsters – but some are in a more Greek archaic style and probably thereby betray the hands of their makers;

8 LEFT Silver alabastron from Usak, with animals and fighting scenes.

9 BELOW Impression from a chalcedony seal showing a 'Mistress of Animals' in Greek style. (Bowdoin College 484. After *GGFR*. W. 20 mm)

they carry more realistic animal forms or 'Greek' goddesses with animals [9]. Many feature small linear devices, presumably personal badges, closely related to those seen designating (we think) construction workmen or teams in the Persian palaces, and related to other eastern practices – such as horse-branding with '*tamga*' symbols, and the like.[43]

The homeland Greek engravers, notably in Ionian areas, whether or not under the Persian yoke, had been turning towards a new seal shape – the 'scaraboid' – also derived from Babylonia, with a plain domed back, less archaic decorative detail (like borders), certainly without any scarab-beetle detailing of the back, and larger. They appear throughout the 'Persian period', and beyond, and accommodate some remarkable studies, even approaching portraiture for heads, but were especially concerned with animal subjects. A very large class of these seals has been identified as 'Greco-Persian' and their original home is likely to have been Anatolia and the artists mainly Greek or certainly Greek-trained.[44] They were widely distributed, some found even in Italy but also, especially in later versions, into Central Asia and as far away as Ceylon, after the fall of the empire. Those of imperial Persian date carry some purely Persian subjects, but often with a Greek inspiration since they may depict the Persians and their women at play, even love-making, or relaxing in a family setting, scenes never encountered in the imperial arts of Persia but common in the Greek world [10]. A few have purely Greek subjects but, in details of their iconography, are 'foreign', so probably designed far from the Aegean [11]. Most have brilliant animal studies [12, 13]. While the Greek inspiration is clear for the most lifelike of them, on others, for both animal and human figures, the technique is generally less realistic than the Greek; and more use is made of

10 Impression from a blue chalcedony scaraboid seal showing a Persian being served unguent by a woman. (Later inscription, from the Koran). (Oxford, Ashmolean Museum 1921.2. W. 24 mm)

11 Impression from a blue chalcedony scaraboid seal from the Punjab showing Herakles stepping over a dead lion to receive a jug from a nymph. 5th cent. BC. (London, British Museum, Walters no. 524. W. 35 mm)

12 ABOVE Impression from a chalcedony scaraboid seal showing a Bactrian camel. (London, British Museum, Walters no. 547. W. 33 mm)

13 RIGHT Blue chalcedony scaraboid seal showing a hyena. (Malibu, Getty Museum. H. 25 mm)

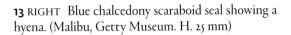

the decorative properties of drill work, long a feature of eastern seal-engraving, but which the Greek artist regularly disguised. So we have here a marriage of styles and techniques, but producing a range of motifs that goes far beyond the usual eastern repertoires. There can be no doubt that it was the presence and influence of Greek artists in Anatolia that accounts for this wave of Hellenic taste in western Persian satrapies. Cognate is the art of the engraver of dies for coins, and coinage was yet another of the Anatolian Greek gifts to the east. The designs for coins progressed from the archaic to the full classical, including portraiture (and in the east possibly sooner than in the homeland), and the result is the production of Greek-style coinage for the Persian subjects. This may bear portraits of Persian satraps [14], or the king himself adopting the pose of an Apollo testing his arrow [15] – a subject with a long eastern history (cf. ill. 51). At home, more often, the Great King of Persia is rendered in traditional pose and style [16].[45] On the great Nereid Monument from Xanthos in Lycia the local king is shown dressed as a Persian, seated under an umbrella, greeting two Greek-clad Greeks.[46]

A genre poorly represented for the period either in Greece or Persia is painting. There are several painted chamber tombs in Anatolia, mainly in the northwest or southwest (Lycia), rendered in a style which blends sub-archaic Greek and oriental as effectively as do the seals. The wooden built-tomb types are in the traditional Lydian/Phrygian style and offer on their painted walls

14 Silver coin of Tissaphernes, a Persian satrap, inscribed BAS ('of the king'?). About 400 BC. (London, British Museum)

15 Silver coin of Datames, Persian satrap of Tarsus, with the king testing an arrow. 378–372 BC. (Oxford, Ashmolean Museum)

16 Gold 'Daric' coin showing the king running. 4th cent. BC. (London, British Museum)

17 Relief from the 'Harpy Tomb' at Xanthos. The king receives a helmet, harpies at either side. (London, British Museum B287. H. 102 cm)

subjects ranging from Greek myth to scenes of Persians fighting 'natives'. To this extent the figures and their dress are often Persian, and their behaviour a mixture of Greek (the reclining symposium), but also closer to Greek archaic (like the horseman and griffin [**PL. IV**]).[47] By the same token there are stone grave reliefs, notably on four-sided monuments, including one where a king is saluted and Harpies carry souls [**17**],[48] as well as many for the nobles of the native kingdoms, where the Persian is barely perceptible and the Greek is strangely translated into a rather indefinable native idiom, especially in Lycia. These have a distinguished Hellenistic succession.[49] Otherwise, in architecture and sculpture, the Greek cities of the coast make no concessions to new rulers or neighbours, and new big classical temples were being built. At Halicarnassus, Herodotus' birthplace, the Carian king Mausolos, a Persian vassal, had built for himself a tomb of oriental aspect with a pyramid atop, but decorated by the finest Greek sculptors of the day, even if not by the galaxy of names invented for the tradition [**18**].[50] The 'Hippodamian' plan for cities with a regular grid of streets, typified at Miletus, would make more sense in the east for 'new' cities than in the Greece of earlier years, where the cities 'grew' from villages. At Daskyleion the satrapal palace seems to have been designed by Greek architects.[51]

18 Reconstruction of the Tomb of Mausolos at Halicarnassus. (Drawn by Peter Jackson)

Before turning to Greek fortunes in other areas of the Persian Empire it is worth reflecting briefly on their status in Anatolia. In early days they had been simply shore-dwellers of relatively little concern to the mainland powers, whose interests were either landlocked or directed to the east. With Croesus the Lydians began to take a very active interest in their Greek neighbours. Their earlier sack of Greek Smyrna showed that they already in some way regarded them as vassals but sharing a culture which was by no means passive – and the interaction produced the first coinage (in the modern sense). Whatever allegiance these eastern Greeks still felt towards the western 'homeland', Olympia and Delphi (there was some measure of Greek religious unity to appeal to, none political), they were no less involved and indebted to their neighbours. It could be argued that Ionian fortunes in the second half of the 6th century BC were largely dependent on Lydian patronage or at least goodwill.[52] Croesus helped pay for (or perhaps paid wholly for) the great Temple of Artemis at Ephesus, dedicated to a goddess who could very easily be regarded as eastern and was portrayed as such. When Persia takes over in Lydia the goddess remains the focus for the Anatolian population, and is mentioned as beneficiary in the Aramaic inscriptions on tomb monuments erected for 'native Anatolian' vassals of the Great King, and decorated in that quaint amalgam of Greek, Lydian and oriental styles which we have remarked already. However much Greek homelanders still regarded their Ionian kin as pure Greek (remember, there was never a united 'Greek nation' as such, but the bond of language and religion counted for a great deal), it is likely that the Greeks of Anatolia could easily take a more detached attitude, no little conditioned by the fact that many of them were paying taxes to Persian courts or being lucratively employed by them. These too were the folk who were being recruited to work in Persia, even to join a Persian army, and however consciously Greek they were, not least in language, they represent a powerful and influential orientalized Hellenic culture that would prove to be the principal guardian of the Greek heritage in arts, thought and administration, however much the cultural and religious appeal of Athens, Sparta, Olympia and Delphi was still acknowledged. Artemis of Ephesus and Apollo of Didyma were no lesser focuses for their Greekness. But, as we have seen, Artemis was already something of an easterner and both

Artemis and Apollo had also served non-Greek religious needs. The Persians had destroyed the temple of Apollo at Didyma and carried off the cult statue (a time-honoured eastern demonstration of control). The Greeks had to guard and propagate their values in the east without Macedonian help, but these were very much the values of semi-orientalized Greeks of Anatolia.[53]

Elsewhere in the Persian Empire, to the south, in Phoenicia, we encounter one of the more remarkable phenomena of the Persians and their subjects and their relationship to Greek arts and artists. Coinage, inevitably, reflected Greece, and both Athenian 'owl' coins and Aeginetan 'turtles' were imitated.[54] The Persians generally did not interfere with local dynasties or their leaders, so long as it was clear who was in charge and tribute was paid. At Sidon especially a type of marble anthropoid sarcophagus had been adopted, based on Egyptian forms as was so much in Phoenicia, over centuries, but with the heads modelled in a manner soon determined by Greek art rather than anything local.[55] Another sarcophagus type, figure-decorated and of rectangular form, was a rarity in the Greek world, but there is a late archaic example in northwest Anatolia (the Troad), where a local Greek prince, but perhaps a Persian vassal, was possibly emulating the great Achilles whose tomb (really Lydian) was still shown there and was receiving attention.[56] This sarcophagus type was adopted in Cyprus, and by the kings of Sidon in Phoenicia. Inspiration and workmanship are almost wholly Greek, except for the earliest (the 'Satrap Sarcophagus'), which betrays something of eastern taste, rather reminiscent of the graecizing works of Cyprus. Soon pure classicism prevails, both for sarcophagi and cult reliefs. The culmination, coming just after the overthrow of the Persian Empire, is the 'Alexander Sarcophagus' [PL. III], a masterpiece of pure Greek style, but where the Greek artist has well reproduced a Persian royal audience scene in paint on the interior of the shield of one of the Persians shown fighting Greeks.[57] This suggests some first-hand knowledge of monuments in Persia itself, to which we now turn.

From their western expeditions the Persians had brought back Greek hostages and prisoners, many of whom they settled in Bactria, south of the River Oxus, an area of which Greeks seemed to have had knowledge from an early date and where they placed the home of one of their gods, Dionysos. There

19 Fragment of a statue from Persepolis bearing a Greek graffito study of a head. (New York, Metropolitan Museum 45.11.17. L. 15.2 cm)

20 Fragment of a stone plaque figuring Herakles, Apollo and Artemis from Persepolis. (H. 13 cm. After *PW*)

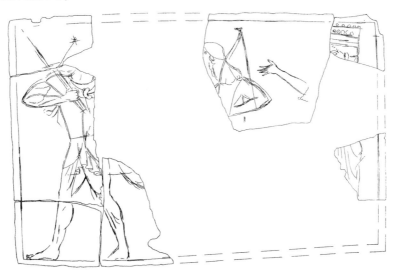

is historical record of a Greek (Sicilian) doctor working at the Persian court, one of the record tablets at Persepolis was inscribed in Greek, and Greeks name themselves in graffiti in the quarries of Persepolis.[58] More to the point, Greek-style figure graffiti appear on Persepolis monuments, not for display but as artists' 'doodles' which would be covered by paint [**19**], and there is even a small stone panel decorated (for painting) with a Greek myth subject in Greek style [**20**].[59] This evidence for Greek artisans and artists in Persia is enhanced one-hundred fold when we look at the architecture and sculpture of the new empire. The sites are revealing. Ecbatana, an old capital, as yet yields little but for a stone lion, early Hellenistic Greek rather than Mesopotamian in style.

21 The tomb of Cyrus (died 530 BC) at Pasargadae. (Photo, author)

Pasargadae was an early centre and was the site of the tomb of Cyrus himself, a gabled building on tall steps, with Greek architectural mouldings at the top of its walls [**21**], and with parallels in Greek Asia Minor and on Thasos in the north Aegean.[60] At the same site are buildings whose columns, with their flutes and turned bases, would not have looked out of place in any Ionian Greek city [**22**] and are quite foreign to a country where decorative stone architecture was totally unknown.[61] The relief sculpture is formal, owing much still to eastern practices (though not practices in Persia, which was innocent of such) but with disposition of dress folds in splaying patterns that copy Greek archaic art of after the mid-6th century, while here and there the body carving is so

22 Column bases of Palace P
at Pasargadae. Late 6th cent.
BC. (Photo, author)

23 Feet from a relief in
Palace S at Pasargadae.
Late 6th cent. BC.
(Photo, author)

elegantly naturalistic as to be paralleled only in Greece [23][62] – totally unlike
the heavier patterned forms of the Near East, as in Assyria. There must be
Greek hands here. The styles are those which had been met by Cyrus and his
court in the Greek cities of Anatolia, and we may imagine that he brought
back with him artists and craftsmen in a deliberate attempt to create for his
new empire an architectural tradition of its own. Darius completes the project
repeating the same graecized forms, at Susa and Persepolis.

Darius' 'Foundation Charter' for Susa lists the places in the empire from
which he got materials and labour: 'The men who wrought the stone, they
were Ionians and Sardians. The men who wrought the gold, they were Medes
and Egyptians. And the men who worked on the wood, they were Sardians and
Egyptians. The men who worked on the baked brick, they were Babylonians.

And the men who adorned the wall, they were Medes and Egyptians'. So this was a construction programme which recruited the styles and skills of the whole empire, and for what we see most of – the 'stone' – Ionians and Sardians (Lydians) are named.[63]

After Pasargadae the other major imperial cities are Susa and Persepolis, the latter built on a new site. The name Persepolis was only applied after it fell to Alexander; the Greeks knew it as Persai. Susa was at least as impressive, but on an old Elamite site and somewhat less completely known (but long studied by French archaeologists and with a large selection of its architectural and decorative arts visible in the Louvre).[64] What appears to have happened in the early 5th century was that a team of artists, probably at the behest of Darius himself, devised architectural and sculptural plans, details and forms which were to dictate the appearance of monumental Persian art until the end of the empire. The sources were largely Greek but with much also from other areas of the empire, the architectural arts of Egypt (some capital forms, the cavetto moulding and glazed decoration – for which there was a more remote Elamite precedent), and Mesopotamia (not architecture or style but the physical forms of royal and divine male heads and some monsters). Building plans tended to the hypostyle – a sea of columns for broad buildings – for which a precedent might be found in the supports for ambitious nomad tentage in Central Asia but which, rendered in stone, resemble rather more Egypt and the deep colonnades of Greek temples, as at Ephesus. The use of carved stone for such architectural elements is a first for Persia. The columns are fluted in the Greek manner, their capitals with both Greek and Egyptian mouldings, as well as some borrowed from furniture, making for a more top-heavy appearance than that apparent in the Greek world, though not unlike Egypt. The bases present a medley of Greek and oriental decorative forms [24]. They were to support a flat ceiling of wooden beams, so the overall aspect of any Persian capital was quite unlike that of any Greek town or sanctuary.

There is plentiful use everywhere of the Greek carved ovolo ('egg-and-dart') and related mouldings ('bead-and-reel'). The human figures adopt the late archaic Greek style of splaying dress, even when it sometimes contradicts the non-Greek all-over patterns of colour, as on the Susa soldiers [PL. V] where

24 Base from the Apadana at Persepolis. 5th cent. BC. (Photo, author)

the overlying geometric pattern contradicts the realistic, graecizing carving beneath. We have remarked how the presence and use of foreign craftsmen is attested by Darius' 'Foundation Charter' inscription found at Susa, which names the sources of materials and craftsmen from all over his empire. A nice example is a statue of Darius himself [25], of Egyptian stone and once set up in Egypt, but taken in antiquity to Susa, where he is shown in Greek-style dress, but four-square and with a back-pillar in the Egyptian manner, with Egyptian and cuneiform (Persian) texts and illustration of subject peoples in the Egyptian manner. His head, missing, was most probably more Mesopotamian in aspect.[65] Similar graecizing folds appear in the dress of a fragmentary stone statue of a woman from Susa.[66]

What is remarkable, and totally at variance otherwise with the development of Greek art, which through the 5th century BC rapidly moved on to the full 'classical' style, is that in Persia the conventions agreed and invented in the early 5th century and most fully displayed at Persepolis remained virtually unchanged – presumably deliberately so – except in trivial detail, to the end of the empire, by which time Greek art was moving on from the pure classical into the Hellenistic. Thus, by around 460 BC, Greek artists were already abandoning the geometry of late archaic folded dress; a good example is the marble statue of 'Penelope' at Persepolis, presumably there as either loot or

a gift [**PL. VI**].[67] These developments, which depended on a radically different approach to representation and were abetted by new techniques, notably in bronzework, were studiously ignored in Persia, although not in their empire. In a way they mirror other manifestations of the Greek way of life, the importance of the individual, even democratic values, of little concern to imperial Persia. And there are other Greek and foreign objects in Persia, also acquired by conquest or as gifts from the vassal states whose servants are seen in procession on the Persepolis reliefs with their token gifts of tribute in their hands, or supporting the royal throne. Minor works in ivory also often bear a very Greek stamp and may have been made by Greeks, including part of an ivory rhyton with a siren and palmettes.[68] The Persians were not much respecters of foreign persons but their

25 Statue of Darius from Susa (once in Egypt). (Teheran Museum)

artists were often open to influences from foreign arts. And Greeks – craftsmen, scribes, doctors, workmen, slaves – became a familiar presence alongside
the permitted immigrants from other areas of the empire.

The view from home

Greece had escaped physical domination by the Persians, except along the
coast of Anatolia. However, their awareness of the arts and behaviour of the
easterner, Persians included, was heightened. It is possible to overestimate
this effect since it manifested itself most in attitudes, such as that towards
and in favour of luxury products, which might easily have happened in other
ways, and had partly already through contact with the Lydians. Moreover,
Greek artists had long been accustomed to copying, even if only in details,
eastern decorative forms and shapes. Thus, although there are several 'Persian'
features adopted for Athenian pottery they represent a very tiny proportion of the production overall. The basic shapes of clay cups used in Athens
were essentially eastern metal forms to which the Greeks had added feet and
handles, a mode preferred in the west while the east used smaller handleless
cups, as we have already observed. Certainly Persian wealth counted for no
little and Greek states courted the Persians for this reason. Upper classes
may have aped some Persian manners in the dining room and on the hunting
field. But on the ground little changed. A few oriental items of dress had a
short vogue – sleeved jackets (the *kandys*) and the like – and Persian decorative schemes are seen on some monuments where we may be sure that there
was some direct connection with Persian influence or patronage. Thus, from
north Greece are ivory relief plaques showing Persians as in a Greek court
and at a Greek symposium.[69] Of the Persian invasions of Greece no real trace
remained beyond the ruined buildings and walls that had to be rebuilt. There
were no great Persian cemeteries – after the battle of Marathon the bodies of
the Persian dead were thrown into a pit.[70]

There are more unusual monuments to Greek and Persian relations
revealed in the commonest preserved medium for figure representations in
the Greek world of this period – vase painting. There are several 5th-century

scenes of Greeks fighting Persians, and some of Persians alone where they are regularly depicted as almost comic figures, even the butt of obscenity [PL. IX].[71] This is no more than we might expect in a popular art practised for a population whose main experience of the Persians was as repelled invaders and which probably exaggerated the scope of their success. But there are also some special products and painters with unusual interests.

One Athenian vase painter, Xenophantos, made an elaborate relief vase in about 400 BC, apparently aimed at the Greco-Persian market in the Black Sea area. It was found in the Crimea and was just possibly even made there. It shows Persian princes hunting monsters in a totally Greek manner, but for the costumes, some weapons and the monsters themselves. This would have made sense only in a very persianized Greek environment and we have no reason to think that Persians were much taken by Athenian red-figure vases. The protagonists are named, some Greek, others historical Persians, princes and satraps, so the whole is an idealized statement of aristocratic Persian and Greek behaviour in a near-supernatural setting [26].[72]

26 Relief/red-figure jug by the Athenian Xenophantos showing Persians attacking griffins, from Kerch, Crimea. (St Petersburg, Hermitage Museum, St 1790. H. 38 cm)

27 Drawing of the decoration on a (Greek) South Italian crater showing the court of the Persian King Darius. (St Petersburg, Hermitage Museum, St 1790)

Farther off, in southern Italy, Greek vase painters had established an important school in Apulia, and in the mid- and later 4th century there were in it artists displaying a peculiar interest in and knowledge of the affairs of Greeks and Persians in the east. It is not easy to find an explanation for the phenomenon, presumably personal, a product of informed travel and observation. From one of them we have our only plausible 'portrait' of the Persian imperial court and Greco-Persian relations, and one very different from the formal Persian presentation of such occasions, since these had a special message. There are several that seem to reflect, even in details of iconography, battles of Alexander's Greeks and Persians, but the Darius Painter's name vase [27] becomes yet more explicit. In its upper register we have a purely Greek scene in which the history of the period is depicted in a form of divine allegory. A personification of Greece is being led into the presence of Zeus and Athena, while a personification of Asia is being enticed from sanctuary by a demon. Below is the Persian court at Persepolis ('Persai'), as never shown so realistically in this or other guise in Greek or Persian art. A messenger in mixed Greco-oriental garb is haranguing Darius, perhaps warning him of impending threats from the west, and the courtiers are dressed, some as Persians, some partly as Greeks, and so presumably from the western satrapies. Worried Persian subjects appeal to the King from below right, and below left is a view of tribute being brought into the royal treasury and accounted by a Greek clerk.[73]

The view from Homeric heritage

Whatever of historicity is deemed to be contained in the Homeric poems about the Trojan War and its aftermath depends no little on the interpretation of Hittite texts which might reveal conflict and that certainly attest what we know from archaeology, that Greek cities were established on the Asia Minor coast in the Bronze Age. When we come to the confrontation with the Persians the real history, and more importantly the mythological tradition, combine to provide antecedents for the conflict that were probably of considerable importance to Greeks and their attitudes to this threat from the east. Herodotus gives a good account of these attitudes, but we must allow for the fact that, being an Asiatic Greek himself (of Caria), he may have taken a more sensitive view of the issues. 'According to the Persians best informed in history', he writes at the start of his *History* (I.1–5), 'the Phoenicians began the quarrel.' They were busy traders in Greece – a fact barely true of the late Bronze Age when the Trojan War was set. The Trojans had kidnapped Io, daughter of Inachos, king of Argos (the prime Mycenaean capital, with Mycenae), and took her to Egypt. Later some Greeks (Herodotus thinks Cretans, who were in fact much exposed to eastern influences in the 9th/8th centuries BC but not, it seems, themselves great travellers) retaliated by carrying off the daughter of the king of Tyre, Europe. Moreover, they went to Aea (Colchis) and carried off the king's daughter thence as well – she was Medea (of the Jason legend). In the next generation the son of King Priam of Troy, named Alexander (Homer's Paris), sought revenge by kidnapping Helen, daughter of the king of Sparta, whence the Greek expedition and the siege at Troy. 'Such is the account which the Persians give of these matters.... Whether the account is true, or whether the matter happened otherwise, I shall not discuss further.'

We may doubt whether this was truly a Persian account rather than, more probably, an Asiatic Greek one. At any rate it provided Greeks with a ready parallel for the Persian Wars and their artists were not slow to equate Trojans of myth history with their new and real eastern enemies, and to depict Trojans as Persians. In the Homeric version the actors are heroic mortals, worked upon by gods and goddesses. In later years mythological reflections of history belong wholly to heroes and gods, as we shall see intermittently in the following chapters, to be brought together as an exceptional and entertaining semi-historical parable discussed in the Epilogue.

CHAPTER 3
Greeks and Alexander 'the Great'

The invasion of the Persian Empire

North of the Greek states lay the Macedonian kingdom. It had been penetrated by the Persian invasions of the early 5th century, and occupied, with no lasting harm done so far as we can judge. The Macedonian language was related to Greek, but remotely, hardly more than to any other Indo-European language, and the Macedonians were not Greeks, did not speak Greek, nor did they write. To the Greeks their coastline was a foreign place on which to plant colonies, just as they did in Italy, but since it was immediately adjacent these soon became the basis for an extension of the Greek 'homeland'.[74]

But Macedonia was rich, in minerals and farmland. Its physical situation was so unlike that of Greece to the south that it naturally prospered as a whole rather than in separate states. Its kings could build palaces and monumental tombs on what seems an Anatolian pattern. They had big ideas. In the 5th century they began to cast covetous eyes abroad and not least on Greece, beginning to absorb, through imitation and migration of artists, much of Greek art and culture, although certainly no form of democracy (rare enough in Greece at any level). The Greeks were typically disdainful of their rich and powerful neighbour and tended to rebuff advances and any attempts to infiltrate through the creation of pro-Macedonian leagues. But the Macedonians admired Greek civilization, as did the Romans in later years, however much they may have despised the Greeks themselves, and they wanted to embrace it, even to be regarded as part of it. Philip II of Macedon (reigned 359–336 BC) united his country and spread its boundaries to the south, expanding or destroying Greek cities. He had little trouble in northern Greece but Athens and Thebes resisted the Macedonians until they were defeated decisively at the battle of Chaeronea in 338 BC, an event celebrated by the erection there of a colossal and very Greek statue of a lion.

Now that Philip could regard himself as an honorary Greek he began to look east, towards an empire that still had more than vestigial interests in the west. His pose, that his mission was to free the Greeks of Asia Minor and exact revenge for the Persian assaults on Greece itself in 480/79 BC, was rather a sham, disguising sheer territorial ambition. But he was ready to appear to be behaving in a pro-Greek manner, despite his attitude and behaviour towards contemporary Greeks. There were some Greeks who were acquiescent, and he was even encouraged to attack Persia by the Athenian lawyer and orator Isocrates. However, Macedonian palace and dynastic intrigues, such as always beset such kingdoms, led to his assassination in 336 BC.

In dealing with ancient and modern attitudes to Greeks and Macedonians we have to remember that we are almost wholly dependent on the testimony of Greek authors, most of whom may have been schooled in believing that Philip's son Alexander was near-Greek and to some degree a saviour and champion of their nation. The attitude persists, and Alexander can be treated as a Greek hero, motivated by the very best and pro-Hellenic feelings, and with an essentially Greek empire. But even the historians' testimony, since they were prone to record the truth, tells a different story. Alexander emerges as a brilliant general, certainly, but a man who mainly despised the Greeks and often acted against their best interests, although he was in many ways dependent on their skills, more administrative than military.

Philip had seen to it that Alexander was brought up to Greek ways, tutored by no less a sage than Aristotle from Athens. It is difficult to imagine what a teenage riding-and-shooting prince could have learned, and the later stories of him mocking his tutor ring true.[75] He spoke some Greek, but even to the Greeks there was always some hesitancy about his authenticity. He was alleged to have had a copy of the *Iliad* annotated by Aristotle in a box[76] – I wonder. However, in the Greek manner he pretended to a legendary Greek heritage, through the heroes Perseus and Herakles, even from Achilles. So his eastern ambitions might seem in a way to be continuing the Trojan War, and indeed he visited Troy to pay respects to 'Achilles' tomb' and pick up 'Achilles' shield'. Elsewhere he might seem to be following the god Dionysos' footsteps into Asia, 'pursuing the Scyths beyond the bounds of Dionysos'; following Herakles too, and both god and hero had an eastern aspect and from an early date. It is clear that Alexander encouraged the view that he could be assimilated to them. His mother Olympias was said to have had a fondness for snakes (like a maenad).[77] This was a mode long familiar in Greece for rulers, but Alexander took it farther, and even embraced a persona as Zeus, after visiting the god's Ammon shrine in Egypt, and thereafter often wearing the Zeus-Ammon rams' horns in portraits. It was an easy step from this to begin to entertain the possibility of his own immortality and to consider the appropriateness of obeisance before him, a Persian practice abhorrent to Greeks and, as it proved, not much to the taste of Macedonians. And after he had occupied the Persian homeland and began to move on east he seems to have been more obsessed with a view of himself as the new emperor of Persia, adopting suitable costume, expecting fitting behaviour from his followers, and acting rather like what the Greeks regarded as a 'barbarian' king, although his elite 'Companions' resisted Persian dress. His attitudes could not have endeared him to many, but he was militarily, and therefore personally, irresistible.[78]

Our principal source for Alexander is the Greek 2nd-century AD historian Arrian, but he had been the subject of many monographs and other histories, of which we have fragments. With Arrian we can follow Alexander's progress through the Persian Empire, to the sack of Persepolis and into Asia. Our best supplementary guide is simply geography, with archaeology (mainly art history) providing a sometimes vivid commentary on events. Arrian was no fool: 'Alexander said that he wished to punish the Persians for sacking Athens and burning the temples when they invaded Greece, and to exact retribution for all the other injuries they had done to the Greeks. I do not think that Alexander showed good sense in this action nor that he could punish the Persians of a long past age' (*Anab.* 3.18.12).

Alexander's army was formidable, unlike Greek armies except in the use of exceptional platoons of hoplite soldiers, with extra long spears (*sarissai*), and in his most intelligent and effective use of cavalry – never a strong point for the Greeks. He crossed the Hellespont to invade the Persian Empire in 334 BC with 40,000 men, of whom only 7,000 were Greek hoplite allies. But there were also Greek mercenaries (5,000) and Balkan troops, and the whole force rose to well over 60,000 within four years, and later, some have thought, even doubled. In Asia Minor he was often facing Greeks in Persian service and could reflect that they were in fact traitors to the Hellenic ideal, though they were clearly happy and prosperous enough as the distant king's vassals. They suffered for it.

In Alexander's campaigns his Greeks seem to have played no prominent role, and the forces from the Corinthian League, which had been formed to support the Macedonians against Persia, were demobilized after the battle at Ecbatana in 330 BC. He made little enough use of a relatively small Greek fleet of 160 ships and soon dismissed it. Perhaps he was not totally confident in a people so recently defeated by his father, and one of whose major cities, Thebes, he had himself recently (333 BC) destroyed. His triumphant progress through the Persian Empire, and all its provinces, including Egypt, was a Macedonian success, even if proclaimed as avenging the Greeks, whose leadership he had assumed. The Persian Empire was already in some disarray, with several local revolts, generally crushed, but we do not see that the local populations were for the most part glad to be 'liberated' by Alexander. He was an utterly ruthless conqueror, merciless even to his own folk if they crossed him. He was responsible for the arranged deaths of several prominent courtiers and has even been suspected of conniving in his father's murder. It is difficult to admire much in his career beyond his military successes, which were staggering, dismantling the most powerful empire that the world had seen in barely ten years; moreover, this was an empire that, in the terms in which we can understand any ancient empire, seems the most 'civilized' and forward-looking of antiquity. Alexander, in destroying it, has a lot to answer for, but he incidentally helped carry Greek manners, arts and peoples far to the east, and this is our concern.

Into Asia

Alexander's armies marched beyond Persia into Central Asia, encountering native as well as Persian resistance in the outlying satrapies. The Persians had perhaps never been such harsh masters; after all they had come from Central Asia in the first place and were, in a way, 'at home'. They had built towns, fortresses and palaces in the east, and the Persian stamp remained long visible on culture. His campaigning became more and more ruthless, conspiracies against him multiplied, and his behaviour became even less like that of an avenger of Greeks. He married a Bactrian princess, Roxane. His victorious surge ranged wider, north to the Syr Darya, soon south into India itself, and it seemed that even the boundaries of the known world were too small for him. At length his men could stand no more and refused to go yet farther south and east, and Alexander had to acknowledge that his vicious campaign of revenge and acquisition was at an end, and he turned for home. But behind him he left an organization based on what the Persians had established, with 'satrapies' which had been managed by Persian officials and no doubt some Greek staff. His determination to 'settle' Asia as part of his new empire is shown by his desire to found cities, new Alexandrias like the one in Egypt. Not all the alleged foundations can be identified and the record of them may be inflated, as well as confused.[79] Likewise there is seldom any consensus about the composition of the population of the new cities – locals, retired Greek and Macedonian soldiers, their camp-followers;[80] these were by no means normal Mediterranean *poleis* in their organization or personnel, yet they certainly contributed to some settled way of life for many Greeks, and in various respects echoed the appearance and structure of Mediterranean towns. But Alexander could pretend that he (as if Greek) could find himself at home, and at Nisa it was said that the Indians surrendered to him because their city had been founded by Dionysos and was the only place where ivy grows (Arrian, *Anab.* 5.1).[81]

Persians had already settled Greek prisoners and hostages in Bactria, from their 5th-century campaigns, mainly in Anatolia (notably the people of Didyma, the Branchidai). These had become bilingual and, to a degree, possibly degenerate, depending on your point of view – perhaps simply accustomized to a new environment and neighbours. They were partly responsible for some local minting of Greek-type coinage, beside the Greek-inspired Persian, introducing an influential form of monetary economy just as the Greeks had done in the western Mediterranean. When Alexander found these Greeks in the east he killed them 'for the crimes of their ancestors', perhaps regarding them also as traitors – there were, after all, more Greeks in the Persian army than in Alexander's, where most were mercenaries rather than patriots from a united

28 Silver decadrachm coin of Alexander the Great, showing him as Zeus with a thunderbolt and Victory overhead, and on the reverse Alexander (?) attacking an Indian war elephant. Minted in Babylon (?) about 323 BC. (Drawing, author)

homeland. So we cannot regard his vengeance for the Greeks, carried so far to the east, as intended to establish new boundaries for Greekness rather than simply the rule of Macedon – yet, perversely, it did. Alexander died in Babylon in 323 BC, and at the news the Greeks in Bactria revolted.

Alexander's heritage in the east is the subject for many pages to come.[82] His success was celebrated in his lifetime in a medium which the Greeks, and especially the Romans, found particularly effective, since it was so easily and widely diffused. In Babylon were struck the coins that show Alexander as the Greek Zeus on one side, holding a thunderbolt and crowned by Victory (Nike, whose image will have a longer life in the east than Alexander's), and on the other a cavalryman, perhaps Alexander again, attacking a war elephant, no doubt that of the Indian King Poros [28].[83] The Alexander image survived long on eastern coins. One remarkable gold example has a rugged portrait of him, wearing the Zeus-Ammon horns, minted in the east and known so far in just

29 Clay head of Alexander, from Hadda.

30 Impression of the gem illustrated in PL. VII, showing the head of Alexander.

one specimen [**PL. VII**], recently recovered, and which has aroused some suspicions (probably wrongly).[84] But the distinctive profile with jutting forehead and scowl became well known, in bronze and clay,[85] and on a remarkable gem cut in a rare stone and concealing a tiny inscription in Indian Kharoshti script [**30**, **PL. VIII**],[86] as well as much elsewhere. Whatever the Greeks thought of him, his image and victories were to haunt their art and history for many years to come, and even far from his and their homelands.

Greeks now found themselves in Asia, having soldiered against or for Alexander, a leader whose assumed Greekness seemed to have been rapidly fading. Earlier Greek knowledge of the region had been very varied. Herodotus had a lot to say about the habits of the nomads there, and the related Amazons, a fighting race of women whom most Greeks probably located in northeastern Anatolia.[87] Greek settling and trading in Colchis (modern Georgia) had led them close to the Caspian Sea and the routes into and from Asia. We have seen how, from the later 7th century on, they had been in touch with the Scythians on the northern coast of the Black Sea and were soon trading vigorously and supplying them with appropriate luxury goods, some modelled on Scythian shapes but in Greek style.[88] In this way Greek art was already beginning to permeate Central Asia, independently of its influence in Persia. Farther south, the presence of Bactrians in the Persian army was twice noted in Aeschylus' play *Persai*, early in the 5th century BC. At the end of that century the playwright Euripides had Dionysos resident in Bactria before returning to Greece,[89] and we have noticed Greeks settled there by Persians. At about that time Ctesias, a Greek visitor to India, remarked on how good the wine and cheese were; this could be a 'home from home'.[90] Ctesias was a doctor attending the Persian court around 500 BC. We know his writings only from the quotations of others, but from them it is clear that at least one Greek had already heard the tales of 'Indian' marvels, the skiapods, the griffins that guard the gold.

Dionysos and Herakles were soon being recruited as proto-Alexanders invading the east. It was said that Dionysos found in the Indus Valley the town of Nisa – the name of his old nurse, and nearby Mount Meru, centre of the Indian universe and covered with ivy and vine, and for him a reference to *meros* ('thigh'), since he had been born from Zeus' thigh. Greek mythography could compass any eventuality when it wished.[91] We shall have to revert to the vinous theme later.

The Greek world-view placed an encircling sea, the Ocean, around their known world, with outlets at the Caspian and around Arabia; of the continents beyond they knew nothing beyond hearsay. They were aware of India, but China lay hidden behind deserts and mountain ranges. Herodotus' detailed description of inner Asia did not depend on first-hand knowledge but was well-founded, much of it corroborated by Chinese sources,[92] and not as fanciful and unreliable as some classical scholars have thought.

The Hellenistic heritage: 3rd to 1st centuries BC

At his death Alexander left an empire that was roughly co-extensive with what the Achaemenid Persian kings had ruled, but including Greece, however uneasy many of the Greeks may have felt about it.[93] The empire's geography broadly followed what Persia had established, but local rule depended on the presence and armies of Alexander's generals, soon to develop into a nexus of independent but competing kingdoms ('kingdoms' being a Macedonian concept foreign to Greek thought and preferences). Although essentially a Macedonian empire, it bore much appearance of being Greek, and its organization depended largely on what Persian rule had established. There were Greeks throughout it already, and many more came flooding in to live, trade and join the administration. This, though managed by 'kings' and 'governors', still had much Greek and Persian about it, and at lower levels there was some degree of democracy, but it would be wrong to think that the eastern Hellenistic world was a logical successor to the classical Greek. Homeland Greece and its western colonies in the Mediterranean still clung to much of the rather chaotic styles of classical political behaviour, and only succumbed to imperial bureaucracy when Rome intervened. In the east the Macedonians remained largely disdainful of Greeks, who had to forge their own fortunes but were pervasive if seldom dominant.

In Egypt the Macedonian Ptolemaic dynasty ruled a country which had welcomed Greeks from the 7th century BC on, and the new city of Alexandria, where the great man was buried, expressed in many ways the essence of the Greekness of Hellenistic arts, subtly wedded to the far longer traditions of Egypt, and ready to feed back into Greece, and Rome, much that was to shape the later development of classical art. The Ptolemies also controlled for a time from Egypt parts of the east Mediterranean seaboard, from Anatolia south, but not being 'Asia' are not further considered here beyond the considerable influence their arts exercised on Greek or hellenized arts in the east.

In Anatolia the Romans had begun their march eastwards, defeating Seleucid Antiochos III, with the help of Pergamum, at Magnesia in 190 BC, leading to the Peace of Apamea in 188 BC. But the Macedonian Attalids came to create a new kingdom centred on Pergamum, soon embracing all Anatolia except Pontus and Cilicia at the east. Attalus III, at his death in 133 BC, bequeathed his kingdom to Rome, and this new Mediterranean power enters the equation for the fortunes of Greeks in Asia. By then the Greek homeland itself had already abandoned any semblance of independence and freedom to Rome, as had the Macedonian kingdom. But in the northeast, after Attalus III, Pontus takes the centre stage, having been modest in expansion locally until the spectacular reign of Mithradates VI 'the Great' (reigned 120–63 BC).

This Mithradates, sharing a name with many easterners and recalling their worship of Mithras, was himself son of a Persian king but claimed also, perhaps rightly, some trace of Macedonian royal blood. He has enjoyed a mixed reputation, as a brave champion of Greeks against the spread of Rome, or as a near-mad monster, obsessed with his own importance and power, and prey to strange religious practices and experimentation with poisons. His ancestry meant that he could pose as a champion of both Greece and the east against the new Mediterranean power. If we discount the bad press he got in antiquity, he emerges as a sad but heroic figure, and he plays an important role in understanding the destinies of the Greek populations of Anatolia.[94]

Having introduced Mithradates I have to anticipate some aspects of other Greek fortunes in Anatolia. Rome started to interfere in Pontus in 89 BC, was defeated, and in the following year Mithradates ordered the massacre of all Romans in Anatolia (some 80,000 of them). The year after he turned west to liberate Greece from Rome but was rebuffed by the Roman general Sulla. A Second 'Mithradatic War' pushed back the Romans, with Mithradates looking to encourage sedition even in Italy itself. The Third War (73–63 BC) sees the Roman Lucullus in Anatolia and Mithradates seeking the support of the Parthians, the new rulers of Persia. The Roman Pompey (the Great) put an end to his ambitions and Mithradates killed himself in 63 BC. Pompey's triumphal procession in Rome in 61 BC, displaying the loot of Anatolia, signalled the end of Greek pretensions to remain in complete control of their own fate, at least to as far as the Euphrates. But it also displayed no little that depended on Greek views about triumphal processions from the east of their homeland, and especially the Dionysos/Alexander associations.[95] Pompey wore what he took to be Alexander's cloak.

We now return to the years immediately following Alexander's reign. Farther east there had still been fighting in Mesopotamia after Alexander, and in 312 BC Macedonian Seleukos captured Babylon, and his dynasty had to try to command territories from the Mediterranean to India.[96] This was, of course, impossible, but cities could be founded and a population imported, as at the new Antioch-Persis established on the Persian Gulf and peopled from western Anatolia.[97] On the Euphrates Apamea and Seleukia faced each other across the river. On the Tigris a new Seleukia effectively replaced old Babylon, 40 miles (65 km) away, and a new Susa was founded at the old Achaemenid capital. Farther northwest, on the Euphrates, near prehistoric Mari, stood a new city, Dura Europos, which in the 2nd century became a major centre, but, for the rest of its history, mainly under Parthian control although heavily aware of the Mediterranean, and to become almost the easternmost point at which Rome had some influence and presence.[98] In the Persian Gulf a town and garrison was established on the island of Failaka[99] to control trade; it was provided with monumental buildings that subtly combined the Achaemenid and Ionic. These were Macedonian cities but their appearance and the bulk of their populations were Greek and native.[100]

The Seleucid Empire is not an easy one to assess. It was spared most of the inter-Macedonian rivalries farther west and had to deal mainly with local populations, Persians, the remnant of the highly organized Persian Empire, and what Alexander had begun to make of it.[101] In Anatolia the further hellenization of an already fairly mixed population continued apace, as at Sardis.[102] Seleukos I rebuilt the Temple of Apollo at Didyma, but with oddly eastern, even 'fire-temple', features, and it continued to serve Anatolian peoples of mixed religions and allegiances.[103] When Seleukos I sent presents to the new temple they included Greek plate, a 'barbarian wine-cooler' and spices from India.[104] Where Alexander went beyond the Persian homeland, to the east, the Seleucids inherited the problems met by both Persians and Alexander. Seleucid

arts were Hellenistic Greek as devised for Macedonian kingdoms living a
Greek cultural heritage, marked by Macedon only to the extent that there
were now important dynastic aspirations to satisfy and not just local Greek
pride. Naturally, in a Persian environment which had absorbed more than a
little of Greek manners, especially in the arts, we find a continuation of much
the same blend, as in the architecture at Failaka. But the Seleucids were very
conscious of being heirs to the Babylonian and Achaemenid empires as much
as to Alexander's, and could be as diligent in the rebuilding of temples near
Babylon[105] as they were in redefining the east as an extension of the 'classical' Mediterranean, Greek and Macedonian world. Thus, brick and terracotta
remain as media even for the monumental, in the old Mesopotamian tradition.
The Hellenistic gold wreaths and other goldwork so familiar from Macedonian
tombs became equally familiar in the east. Some eastern capital cities such as
Uruk were, however, barely affected by the west. In some respects this was the
result of a policy of non-intervention, and the Seleucid east no more became
'Greek' or even 'Macedonian' than India became 'British' in the 19th century.[106]
Seleucid armies too were no more Greek than Alexander's had been.[107] But in
the east, as in Egypt, we need not think that the arts that served the rulers
were other than mainly Hellenistic Greek (there is no 'Macedonian' art or
literature), devised for Macedonian royalty, but still for a partly Greek population, although in a foreign environment to which, however, they had been long
accustomed. The subject of this book sadly has to exclude full consideration of
the evidence for oriental continuity in the arts, except where something Greek
intervenes or merges.

A new problem had been posed by yet another wave of newcomers from
Central Asia, from just east of the southern Caspian Sea: the Parni – Parthians,
their name derived from the Seleucid satrapy Parthava, and starting a dynasty of
their own (the 'Arsacid') in 247 BC. They spread rapidly through old Persia, but
were thrust back at the end of the 3rd century by the Seleucid King Antiochos III
('the Great'; reigned 223–187 BC), who went on to retrace Alexander's steps even
as far as India. After the mid-3rd century the Seleucid hold on the east began
to unravel. This was partly through the defection of the Bactrian Greeks, on
whom more later, although even there a measure of Seleucid control must be

admitted, especially under Antiochos III, and partly through the resurgence of the Parthians under their new king, Mithradates (a common regal name, acknowledging the god of Persians and others). He died in about 138 BC. His empire had become, at least in the east, as extensive as the Achaemenid Persian had been. But his successors had to fight to retain Babylonia, while the Greeks in the east were forging their own new kingdom. Parthian fortunes rallied for a while, before dealings with the grecophil Mithradates of Pontus (see above) and their confrontation with Rome. What we need to consider is the extent to which Greek presence and Greek influence affected the development and appearance of the new Persian/Parthian world of the 3rd to 1st centuries BC.[108]

Yet farther east the story remains more Macedonian/Greek. Seleukos I had been given five hundred elephants by the Indian King Chandragupta (Sandracotta, to the Greeks), in return for control of Kandahar. Elephants, with new types of chariot, had been adapted for use in the traditional Macedonian army, the westerners adding a turreted howdah making them more like tanks.[109] Seleukos' army included many 'natives', while the Greek proportion remained modest. He was fighting Chandragupta in 305 and 303 BC, but eventually the Indian king was left in control of Arachosia and what is now east Afghanistan. At Kandahar his grandson, Mauryan Asoka, left an edict in Greek and Aramaic enjoining Buddhist righteousness (*dhamma*) and forbidding the killing and eating of living things.[110] Alexander's site at Merv (Margiana) was reshaped and fortified by Seleukos' son Antiochos I.[111] But by the mid-3rd century Seleucid rule in Bactria and parts of Parthia was threatened by both natives and Greeks, as we shall see. Kandahar was Alexander's 'Alexandria in Arachosia', but we still know too little of its Greek history despite British excavations, aborted by the Russian invasion in 1978. The site is spectacular, encompassed by great cliffs with, at its centre, the massive mudbrick remains of a citadel, 18th-century in its latest phase, but embracing the ruins of a massive Achaemenid Persian fortress [**PL. XI**].[112] Around 275 BC a Greek inscription records a dedication by a son of Aristonax.[113] Some time in the 2nd century BC one Sophytos had inscribed there, 'at the road side', an acrostic poem in Greek (the first letters of each line give his name and parentage) recording his devotion to culture, but notably his success in leaving home to make a fortune through trade, and returning to

I ABOVE A gold comb from a tomb at Solokha. A Greek cavalier in full armour is being attacked by two Scythians wearing their tight dress and carrying semicircular shields; a fallen horse lies beyond them. Set on a plinth with crouching lions. 5th century BC. (St Petersburg, Hermitage Museum)

II BELOW A gold cup of eastern shape from a tomb at Gaimonova. The decoration is in Greek style: two Scythians seated at ease, a Greek leaf-and-dart pattern above. 4th century BC. (Kiev Archaeological Museum)

III TOP A detail from the 'Alexander Sarcophagus' found at Sidon in Phoenicia. A fight of Greeks against Persian horsemen, the figure at the left probably representing Alexander. Late 4th century BC. (Istanbul Museum)

IV ABOVE A clay relief revetment from a temple at Duver in Anatolia. A horseman in Anatolian dress is pursuing a griffin, in a provincial graecizing style. Early 5th century BC. (Ankara Museum. After Akurgal)

V Stone relief in bricks from the Persian capital at Susa. It shows a warrior with bow, quiver and spear. The painted geometric decoration of his dress contradicts its carved Greek-style natural folds, shown in the drawing below. 5th century BC. (Paris, Louvre)

VI Marble statue of a seated woman from Persepolis, probably representing the mourning Penelope. This was likely a gift from a vassal Greek state to the Persian king. Late 5th century BC. (Teheran Museum. Photos below, author. H. 85 cm)

VII Gold coin from a hoard in Afghanistan. It bears a portrait of Alexander wearing an elephant cap and with the ram's horn signifying assimilation to Zeus Ammon at his ear. Late 4th century BC. (After Holt and Bopearachchi)

VIII Elbaite (like tourmaline) gemstone showing the head of Alexander with the Ammon horn. A tiny inscription in Indian Kharoshti script is at his neck, so it was made in the east (see ill. **30**). Late 4th century BC. (Ashmolean Museum, Oxford 1892.1499. 25 × 25 mm)

IX Athenian red-figure jug showing a Greek sexually threatening a cowering Persian. Late 5th century BC. (Hamburg, Museum für Kunst und Gewerbe 1981.173)

OPPOSITE

X ABOVE Reconstruction of the interior of the Great Hall at the Parthian capital, Nisa, with free-standing and engaged classical columns. 3rd/2nd century BC. (After Invernizzi)

XI BELOW A view of ancient Kandahar from the south, the site of the Persian fortress at the centre. (Photo, author)

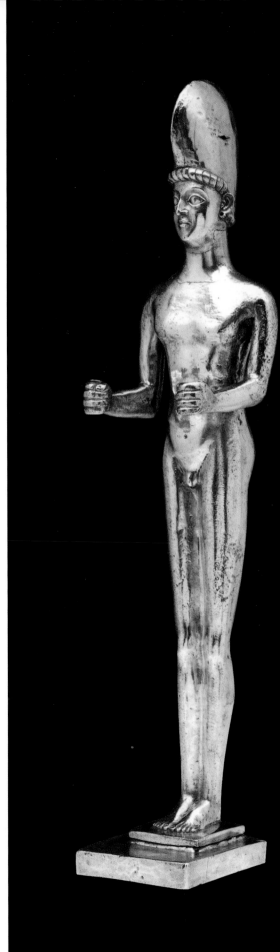

XII Silver statuette of a naked man, with gilt headdress, his hands held forward as if to hold sceptres or branches. From the 'Oxus Treasure'. 5th/4th cent. BC. (London, British Museum WA 123905. H. 29.2 cm)

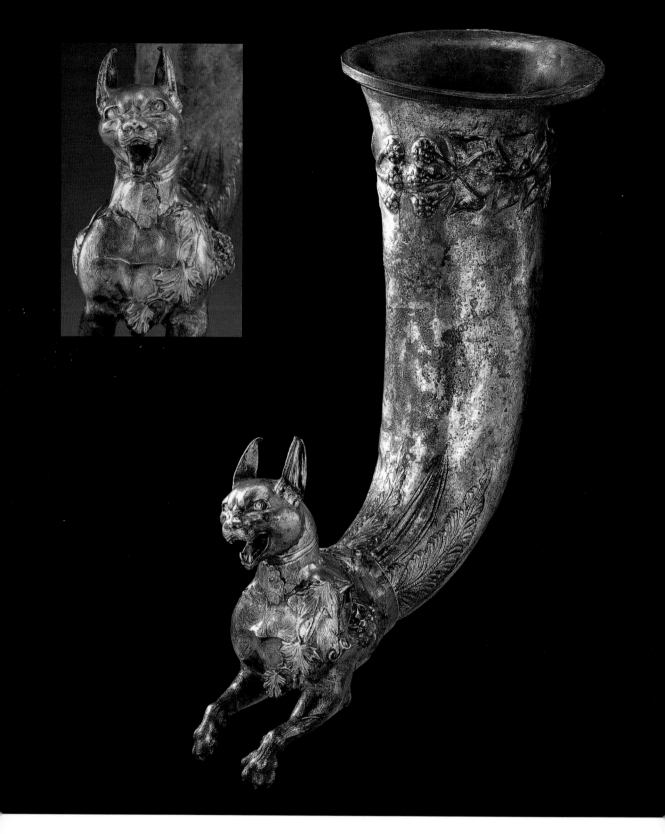

XIII Gilt silver rhyton-cup, a grape vine at the neck, palmettes and buds behind the forepart in the form of a leaping lynx. 3rd/2nd cent. BC. (Miho Museum, Shigaraki. L. 44 cm)

rebuild his family seat and tomb. But Sophytos, through his name and that of his father Naratos, must be seen to be of an Indian family, yet proud to declare his successful career in Greek.[114] And of about the same date a Greek poem dedicated to Hestia and Tyche is found in Tadjikistan.[115]

Coming much later, by 51 BC the Parthians controlled everything from their original homeland, through Persia, into Mesopotamia as far as the River Euphrates, whence they had repelled the Romans in the greatest catastrophe for Roman arms of all time (or so it seemed) at the battle of Carrhae (53 BC). From the 3rd century BC on they had found themselves heirs to both the Achaemenid Persian Empire and the fluctuating Seleucid/Macedonian Empire. The latter poses the usual question about how much is Macedonian, how much Greek, since it is clear that there was no total fusion and there is record enough, also under the Seleucids, of considerable friction between the nominal conquerors and their mercenary or vassal Greeks, who in effect may well have run much of the empire but not the army, and were certainly the major influence in the arts. The Parthians had still to deal with occasionally resurgent Seleucids, and soon, to the east, the new Greek kingdom in Bactria.

To the west, Dura Europos on the Euphrates flourished under the Parthians. It was a Seleucid foundation, occupied by Parthians after about 100 BC, and thereafter, until Sasanian times, offering as rich a mixture of cultures and arts as any city in the Near East, being on the western crossroads of west and east: Christianity, Judaism and Mithraism were all at various times accommodated, with adjusted classicizing arts serving them, notably in painting and mosaic.[116]

The Parthian capital in their homeland, east of the Caspian, was at Nisa, and as early as the 3rd century BC there seems to have been considerable new building there, to suit the home of new dynasties. The *iwan*, a broad open room, open at one side, was a characteristic feature, but at Nisa now much of the architectural carved detail is indebted more to the Greek tradition than to any Persian [PL. X]. When we deal with architecture the ground plans tell as much or more about cultural affiliations, commonly eastern, than the above-ground ornament, which is often Greek-inspired. But in the other arts too, including painting, as at Nisa, Hellenistic styles are developed, clearly by Greek artists working in the east, but often for new masters.[117] Statuary types are very

31 Acrolithic statue of Aphrodite (the dress rendered in poorer stone), from Nisa. 2nd/1st century BC (?). (After Invernizzi)

32 Statue of a goddess in classical archaizing style, from Nisa. 1st century BC. (After Invernizzi)

33 Clay head of a warrior, from Nisa. 2nd/1st century BC. (After Invernizzi)

34 Bronze cheekpiece from a helmet decorated with a winged warrior with tendril legs. 2nd/1st century BC. (After Invernizzi)

Greek – an acrolithic Aphrodite [**31**] (her lower part carved in inferior stone), an archaistic goddess [**32**], and realistic clay heads [**33**].[118] A cheekpiece from a helmet has a Greek warrior, winged and with a floral below the waist [**34**].[119] Much derives from the homeland styles of the Mediterranean, but in the east there are new traditions, and much that seems to have been created by Greeks there can be seen even to have had its effect back in the homeland.

Another example is furnished by the horn-shaped rhyton, a common eastern drinking vessel. It was known in Greece too, part of the general orientalizing, even somewhat persianizing movement since the 6th century BC. In the eastern 'Hellenistic period' it becomes particularly important, executed in gold and silver (often gilt) and decorated with generally Greek floral patterns on the horn and highly imaginative animal heads and foreparts at the pointed 'mouth'[120] [**35, PL. XIII**]. Occasionally, at the geographical fringes, there

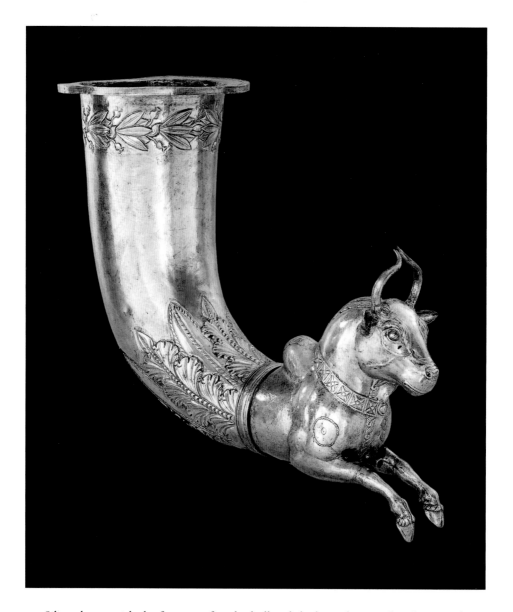

35 Silver rhyton with the forepart of a zebu bull and the horn decorated with a wreath and acanthus leaves. 2nd/1st century BC. (Toledo Museum of Art 88.23)

are clearer indications of recollection of earlier forms for the mouthpieces. But for the majority the pure Greek styles of design and workmanship make clear their sources, even though their customers and patrons may have been Greek, Macedonian, Persian or Parthian. A particularly rich haul of ivory rhyta was found at Nisa, in what looks almost like a butler's pantry, stored ready for the feast. Be that as it may, the workmanship and subjects shown on the rhyta, which also boast relief scenes on their 'collars', are wholly Greek, whether of the new Persian/Parthian world, or, more probably, of the new Greek Bactrian – in which case they are loot. We shall return to them in the next chapter [42–45].

Another field of art of some significance throughout the east is that of seal-engraving. We have looked at the Greco-Persian gems with their mixed subjects. The style and shapes survive the Persian Empire, as do many of the subjects, notably Persian women at ease [36]. But the Persian males disappear and the hunting scenes are conducted by men with flat caps (*kausia*) characteristic of the Macedonians [37],[121] so we may judge them Seleucid. In many respects the style has weakened: there is a lot more simple drill work than there had been even on the Greco-Persian seals, and in no respect do they truly reflect any of the new spirit of the Hellenistic arts of the west. Yet we shall find that they had a following farther east.[122]

Other arts of the 'Hellenistic', intermittently Parthian, east in Persia, are hard to judge since they present a blend of the Greek and eastern in which the latter is often dominant and distorting. A relief carved beside the great Achaemenid relief at Bisitun in Persia, showed (it is largely destroyed now) a king and four vassals in a very stiffly oriental group, albeit in flowing

36, 37 Impressions of a chalcedony scaraboid showing a Persian woman seated with a harp and a dog, and another showing horsemen wearing *kausia* pursuing stags. (Boston, Museum of Fine Arts 03.103; Merz Collection. W. 22 mm and 40 mm)

38 Rock relief at Bisitun showing Herakles (as Verethagna) reclining at feast with his club and quiver. The lion relief below him is older. (After *DCAA*)

Greek-style dress, and one figure holds aloft a totally Greek figure of a trumpeting Victory.[123] Figures of Greek religion and iconography have new roles and identities, and Greek architectural motifs, other than those which had already contributed to Achaemenid Persian art in the palaces, find a new role. All this will be more easily explained when we come to consider Parthia in the Roman period in more detail (Chapter 7), but there is an interesting earlier example of religious/political assimilation which is worth recording. Also at Bisitun in Persia, at the base of the cliff in the gully where Darius had carved his relief and inscriptions, there was a small sanctuary of Herakles, created by a Macedonian for Cleomenes, governor of the 'upper satrapies' in 148 BC. A relief was cut in the rock (just above an earlier outline relief of a lion, appropriately) of Herakles reclining at feast with a cup, his club before him, but also, incongruously (not his weapon), a quiver on the wall above [**38**].[124] For Persians Herakles was Verethagna; there was no problem in borrowing Greek iconography for a Persian god and we shall meet this version of him again.[125] The equation of

Herakles and Verethagna is made explicit in the Greek and Aramaic inscriptions on a fine Hellenistic (about 100 BC) bronze statue of the hero found at Seleucia, but taken there long after it was made, as Parthian booty.[126]

As a finale for the Hellenistic Greek record in the nearer east we may return closer to the Mediterranean, to the kingdom of Commagene, lying between the Euphrates and the coast. The royal house celebrated itself in colossal seated figures, and in reliefs that adjusted Greek realism for an eastern audience more interested in pattern, as in the 1st-century BC relief where a Herakles, again translated as the eastern Verethagna, acknowledges a local king[127] [39], and the monumental idiom of the Greek world again has to compromise with the formality of the east at the hands of, certainly, a non-Greek artist. Generally, Greek traditional figures, not only Herakles, remained popular subjects in all media under the Parthians, but they are

39 Relief slab from Nemrud Dagh showing Herakles/Verethagna with a Commagenian king. (London, British Museum)

sparse and may reflect simply lingering local traditions. And in Commagene there is a plethora of monumental 'Hellenistic' sites, barely explored as yet.[128] Of far more moment for the development of the arts in the region was the new emphasis on frontality for figures, which may still be dressed 'classical' but which abjure the basically naturalistic principles of classical art for something far more formal, and which soon shrink from real portraiture.[129]

CHAPTER 4

The new Greek kingdoms in the east

The kingdoms

We do not know how many Greeks were still living in Bactria in the 3rd century BC, and the Greek realm as 'the land of a thousand cities' is moonshine.[130] The reported numbers, and another reported figure for cities ('twelve'), are suggestive but often conflicting. Very many Greeks (3,000 or 23,000? – sources are confused) had been killed in an uprising after Alexander's death. Relations with those Macedonians who remained behind can only be guessed at, and there must have been much intermarriage with the local population for those who sought a life in the east, just as there must have been numerous 'camp-followers' of various races who had travelled with Alexander's army. Many of the Greeks had probably served with the Persian army, not Alexander's. The Greeks' status in what were still Macedonian/Seleucid satrapies must have been very ill-defined, but they still owed allegiance to the Macedonian king whose behaviour had become more and more oriental. Nevertheless, however much the Greek elements in the east may be denied by some students of Seleucid history,[131] they were there with sufficient numbers and influence to create Greek states and urban cultures which were mainly non-Macedonian/ Seleucid in appearance and behaviour, while Macedonians everywhere were more than ready, like Alexander, to 'cash in' on whatever service or even kudos Greekness might afford.[132]

Diodotos I, the Bactria/Sogdiana satrap, rebelled against Macedonian Antiochos II in the 250s, called himself 'king', and was succeeded by his son Diodotos II, who entered into some sort of pact with the Parthians. (Dates throughout this chapter will not be totally reliable but, within limits, are generally agreed by scholars.) 'Kings' were not much to Greek taste but Macedonian Seleucids had made them familiar. Diodotos II was killed by his satrap (perhaps of Margiana to the south) Euthydemos I in about 235 BC. Both Diodoti minted coins of purely Greek type.[133] Euthydemos reigned until about 200 BC and extended his kingdom south into Aria and Margiana, and north into Ferghana. Around 208 BC he fought off Seleucid Antiochos III, having withstood a two-year siege in Bactra/Balkh. He moved even into Parthia. These were the kings who first established a Greco-Bactrian – becoming 'Indo-Greek' – realm in Asia, and they declared their Greekness with splendid coinage. We may continue to consider their political and imperial fortunes, and any continuing Macedonian presence and activity, before turning to their way of life, their cities and their arts.

Euthydemos sought to consolidate his northern frontiers against movement from north and east, while his son Demetrios I sought rather to expand to the south into India. He even occupied Pataliputra (Patna) for a time, far east along the Ganges, an event recorded also in Indian chronicles.[134] The families and interrelationships of the Greco-Bactrian kings are ground for complicated scholarly discussion, and dependent a great deal on interpretation of their coinage, which we shall consider separately. Their family affairs are not pursued here in detail, but there was another king, Antimachos, who called himself god (*theos*), active in the south, who probably crossed the Hindu Kush and who even minted square coins of Indian type, while a Demetrios II minted bilingual coins. The latter moved farther southeast, into Gandhara ('Gadara' was a Persian satrapy), but was defeated by another northern satrap-turned-Greek king, Eukratides, whose rule began about 171 and lasted until around 155 BC. Other kings of about this time are the brothers Pantaleon and Agathokles, challenging Eukratides from the northeast. It was Agathokles who was the first Greek king to occupy the city of Taxila, whose fortunes are considered below. One thing that is quite clear from the confused record is that the Greek kings spent a major part of their resources and energy fighting or thwarting each other as much as consolidating a real Greek kingdom in the east. In this they were exhibiting that often self-defeating Greek pride and ambition which impeded them from ever becoming a 'world power' politically, as did the Persians, Macedonians and Romans, despite the model of Alexander the Great. And yet, within all this, Greek administrative practices could flourish and provide a secure social basis for life and trade – witness tax receipts, mute testimony to a tight administration.[135]

Their cities and arts

The Greeks, whether under Seleucid or new Greek rule, were described by a Chinese observer in the early 2nd century BC (see below) as living in walled towns, not especially warlike, but busy traders. That sounds quite authentic for Greeks as we know them. They, as had the Macedonians, profited from the extensive and good road system which had been established by the Persians throughout their empire – never a strong point for Greeks. Their towns could not quite be *poleis* in Greek terms, though they might strive to be. Greek buildings and practices could be readily supplied to enhance the Hellenicity – gymnasia, which were as much clubs as exercise grounds, libraries, theatres, stoas and appropriate temples. But oriental religions were strong and well-established, and they could accommodate a degree of Greekness more readily than the Greeks could the oriental. Moreover 'Asian' Greek traditions had had some time to develop for themselves. There were slaves, certainly, but many of other what we would regard as civilizing aspects of Greek life and government became apparent, as indeed they did also in the Seleucid satrapies farther west, for instance, and even in Babylon, where, however, Babylonian law was allowed to remain valid.

Physical evidence for the Greco-Bactrian kingdom(s) down to the later 2nd century BC, when the Greeks were being moved on south, is patchy (except for the coinage) but in places very rich.[136] Their occupation of Bactra/Balkh itself is elusive on such a massive site, which is nevertheless often claimed as the source of various Greek objects. Some 20 miles (30 km) west is a major Persian site at Cheshm-e Shafa, where we might expect more Greek material. Far more important has been the excavation of a whole town founded originally under Seleucid rule but soon a major centre for the Greco-Bactrian 'empire', and lasting until the later 2nd century BC. It is to the east, on the Oxus, at Aï Khanoum (its medieval name, 'Lady Moon'). The site was well excavated by the

French in 1965–78. Much has been published though the site itself has been and is being much disturbed during the current troubles. It was very probably one of the new Alexandrias, just possibly the 'Alexandria Oxiana' mentioned in a text,[137] and certainly an early Macedonian foundation, even if Seleucid rather than 'Alexandrian'. There had been an Achaemenid Persian settlement not far away, as well as the major prehistoric site of Shortugai, which has yielded links with north India (Harappa), and was a market for lapis lazuli, the mineral for which this area of Afghanistan is the major source. There was also nearby a grand Hellenistic farmhouse complex, demonstrating a very busy market in corn. Aï Khanoum was an early foundation to be occupied by the Bactrian Greeks, and lasted until about 145 BC, when the Greeks were displaced by the ex-nomad Yuehzhi (on whom much more, below).[138]

The town lay in a good defensive position on the Oxus, at the point where it is joined by the Kokcha River from the southeast. There is a distinct flat-topped acropolis, 60 metres (200 ft) high, and a broad lower town along the Oxus, all substantially fortified and roughly triangular with mile-long sides. The character of the buildings and details of the architecture are essentially Greek but idiosyncratic in detail, the result of distance from contemporary Hellenistic architecture and town planning, and of a certain distinctiveness among the Bactrian Greeks, which appears too in other arts, here and elsewhere. The monumentality of the fortifications and palace attest the Macedonian taste, which had been carried east by Alexander and his subjects. The full excavation of Aï Khanoum and what it has taught us is an object lesson on how little we still know about the archaeological history of southern Central Asia, since a single site can so substantially adjust and expand our knowledge and expectations [40, PLS. XV, XVI].

The canonical buildings for a classical Greek *polis* are there. A temple, dedicated to the founder (Kineas) as it would have been in a Greek colonial foundation in the Mediterranean, a gymnasium, a theatre that could serve also as a place of assembly, a palace – since royal trappings are by now respectable among Greeks, at least so far away from home, although the palace plan owed most to eastern practice with series of courtyards. Monumental classical stone architecture with the usual orders (Doric, Ionic, Corinthian) was rather

40 The site of Aï Khanoum at the junction of the Oxus and Kokcha rivers.

foreign to these parts but soon embraced. Neither house nor temple plans quite conform to the Greek model, though the courtyard remains an important element in the houses, even if not set centrally. The temples, although dedicated to Greek deities, follow a more eastern plan, with a central cult room and statue, with side chambers or niches, flat roofs and no exterior sculpture. The prominence of stepped platforms is decidedly Persian – indeed column bases taken from the nearby Achaemenid town were reused.[139]

Monumental sculpture is found too, as well as all the luxury crafts of metalwork, and the 'minor arts' so conspicuous in all Greek towns - clay figurines, decorative revetments for buildings. The relative lack of fine stone, the preferred marble, for sculpture, meant often using the acrolith technique met also in other peripheral Greek sites in the west, with clothed parts of figures carved in wood and only the flesh parts in stone. Stucco is much in evidence, as it was in Parthia, for sculpture and reliefs. Pebble mosaics were made, something of a novelty even in the west at that date. In most respects the quality and style live up to the best of the homeland despite the overall foreign aspect of the town and its setting, a character revealed mainly in details in the arts. There could be no mistaking Aï Khanoum for a replica of Mediterranean life, but equally its Greekness was abundantly apparent, and not least in the inscriptions. There are papyrus fragments with texts from a philosophical dialogue and a play;[140] dedications in the gymnasium;[141] receipts and contents lists painted on jars, including records of payments in Indian coins and in olive oil[142] and 'cinnamon'[143], the last recalling the old dedication on Samos (above, p. 7); and an inscribed stone in the *heroon* of Kineas, given by a Klearchos to remind the far-flung Greeks of the Delphic maxims:[144]

> 'as a child be well-behaved;
> as a youth be self-controlled;
> in middle age be just;
> in old age be wise;
> at death grieve not.'

Eukratides was no doubt the last ruler of Aï Khanoum, and he was a busy warrior to the south. A relic, perhaps, is a strange Indian disc composed of shell, embellished with gold and glass, depicting an Indian scene, and perhaps story.[145] And no less memorable but not wholly Greek, a gilt silver disc [**PL. XIII**], apparently wrenched from furniture (perhaps loot from another site),[146] depicting the Greek goddess Kybele, who was not without eastern connections, in her lion chariot driven by Victory, attended by long-cloaked priests, holding an umbrella and making offerings on a high platform in a rocky landscape overlooked by the sun, moon and a star. Yet, however Greek parts of this look, it also bears the stamp of a craftsman far from home and of a non-Greek setting. More wholly Greek is a small ivory roundel with the relief figures of Aphrodite seated, flowers and a Victory, a relic salvaged from the now robbed site.[147]

Nothing has as yet been found to match this urban site in the rest of the Greco-Bactrian homeland, but there are tantalizing finds which do more than hint at a Greek presence, quite apart from what we shall find of their heritage here and to the south.

Far to the west along the Oxus is Takht-I Sangin, a temple site sometimes known as the Temple of the Oxus.[148] This is because there was found there a small bronze statuette of a Greek satyr [PL. XVIII], playing pipes, on a base that carried a dedication in Greek by Atrosokes (a Persian name) to 'the Oxus', and another apparent inscription naming an Oxus deity. This is perhaps enough to declare the whole complex an 'Oxus Temple'. The parallel with the Anatolian river named after a satyr (Marsyas) is not cogent since in that case the inspiration was a local name and myth.[149] However, an Achaemenid finger ring from the Oxus Treasure (see below) carries an inscription which has been read as Wacsh ('Oxus').[150] At any rate, these are poignant associations of Greek, Persian and locality. The building itself is odd, more like an eastern (Persian) fire-temple.[151] A large courtyard leads to a broad entrance hall (*iwan*), into a four-columned sanctuary, with many smaller rooms around. Architectural details are certainly hellenizing but perhaps more like the Parthian versions of the classical than the Greek.

Many finds certainly go back to the Greco-Bactrian period, with the expected odd mix of Greek and local, but most were recovered from levels that are certainly post-Greek. An interesting combination of styles is often shown. Thus, an ivory scabbard [PL. XIX] copies a Median/Persian form that goes back to the 7th century BC.[152] The creature curled at the chape terminal and the lion are related to the Mesopotamian and Persian but the border of tongue and cable, and the very naturalistic stag, are Greek. On a sword handle [41] the subject, in a Greek style, is Herakles beating down an elderly opponent;[153] and on a part of a scabbard [PL. XXII] a Greek-looking fish-lady holds an oar and a fruit (?) but is also winged and has horses' forelegs[154] – but for the human forepart she would pass as a Greek hippocamp, and might do as well as a personification of the Oxus as the satyr,[155] but we shall find another candidate for that honour. A smaller ivory [PL. XXI] presents a Herakles head in a form not unlike that used for Alexander on coinage.[156] Along with these luxury items are pieces of realistic clay statuettes, near-portraiture and other Greek and Asian trivia. While the architecture and function of Takht-I Sangin must be 'native', much of its wealth seems to have depended on access to luxury objects of Greek type, and there is remarkably a considerable hoard of Greek weaponry. I save for last another ivory, the mouthpiece of a rhyton drinking cup in the shape of a lion [PL. XX], close kin to many that are Greek and especially to the

41 Ivory sword handle from Takht-I Sangin showing Herakles beating down an elderly opponent. 3rd cent. BC. (After *Oxus*)

style that appears on metal rhyta with 'Greco-Parthian' associations, which we have already looked at.[157]

We have already mentioned the other ivory rhyta which deserve notice here for their Greekness – the hoard found in the Parthian capital Nisa.[158] The total Greekness of their style but also the determinedly Greek subtlety of their iconography seems to betoken Greek hands and it is perfectly possible that the whole find is booty from a Greco-Bactrian source. They are decidedly luxury items, enhanced with gold, glass and semi-precious stones [42]. The modelled foreparts of the Nisa ivory rhyta include eastern animal subjects derived from Persian art – horned griffins, graecized lions, and, of

42 Ivory rhyton from Nisa, the neck decorated with facing heads and a festive scene, the forepart in the form of a horned griffin. 3rd/2nd century BC. (After Masson/Pugachenkova)

43–45 Scenes on the necks of ivory rhyta from Nisa, showing Greek poetesses and a rustic scene beneath a vine frieze. 3rd/2nd century BC. (After Masson/Pugachenkova)

other animal subjects, elephants – while others are Greek in subject as in style. The acanthus collar on the stems of the rhyta is Hellenistic Greek. The rims are decorated with Greek floral patterns, including egg-and-dart, but often also rows of frontal heads which are rather an eastern and Parthian architectural and decorative feature.[159] The relief friezes below them are purely Greek, and the abstruse character of some of their subjects suggests that they were created in an environment that was fully aware of the minutiae of Greek iconography and not mere copyist. Moreover, they were likely to be for a clientele that understood them. They include mythological scenes, a fine parade of Greek poetesses [43–44], rusticity [45],[160] and scenes of sacrifice in the Greek manner. One carries a dedication to Hestia, in Greek.[161]

Another western site about which less is known is Dilberzin, once a Persian site, but its niched temple walls carry paintings of the heroic Greek Dioskouroi horsemen [46], and in Greek style, not closely datable and not certainly of the main Indo-Greek period, yet fully expressive of Greek style and subject.[162]

Aï Khanoum, Takht-I Sangin and Nisa are all excavated sites, carefully recorded and for the most part published. We can be sure that more will be found – thus, the Hellenistic walls of Samarkand have been identified, along with fortresses, established no doubt by Alexander.[163] In this area (Sogdiana) north of the Oxus, Alexander's generals established control, and this was a zone for Greek settlement, just as it was south of the Oxus.[164] As sources for

46 Painting from Dilberzin showing the Greek heroes, the Dioskouroi, with their horses. 1st century BC (?).

evidence of Greek arts and life in Bactria the few excavated sites are essential, but they are not the only sources. It is characteristic of a country like Afghanistan, and indeed its neighbours, that a majority of finds is going to be made accidentally, and that, given the nature of the geography, they cannot readily be controlled by authority (especially not when 'authority', however defined, is hostile to the religious character of the finds, a common case where 'national' heritage is, as so often, meaningless). Moreover, in a land of massive sites and long occupation it is in the nature of ancient behaviour that much material is collected in hoards, hidden for security, but never recovered in antiquity, though now a major source for the antiquity-hunter – and scholar. Lack of information about provenience and even more lack of certainty about composition of groups, since a dealer may readily enhance a hoard by adding to it from other sources, bedevil attempts to deal in a completely scholarly way with hoard material, but it would be unscholarly to ignore it. Our area has had more than its share of hoard finds over the last century or two, and they are important for our subject.

One in particular has been long known and impinges a little on our view of Greeks in Bactria. It is the so-called Oxus Treasure, now in the British Museum, until recently fully exhibited there, and said to be from a cache found buried in the banks of the Oxus in 1877. It was partially dispersed, then reassembled, an activity that is not reassuring if we are concerned about its unity. The objects are all precious and most are clearly Persian in origin, which does not mean that they come from Persia but that they were collected from a Persian site in Asia and deposited for safety.[165] Most are earlier than Alexander, and one gold scabbard is probably Median of the 7th century BC and perhaps not from the main find at all but added to it.[166] The treasure is likely to have been assembled from different sources.[167] There are Greek pieces too, notably finger rings, which seem 4th-century in date, and therefore not strictly relevant to Greek Bactria, but they are mentioned here because some have thought the whole hoard to be later in date, they are not irrelevant to the record of Greeks and Greek art in the east, and they involve consideration of another hoard of mainly later objects, which are relevant at this point in our narrative. In the Oxus Treasure there are echoes of Greekness even in the Persian objects – a silver statuette of, it may be, a prince, gives him a Persian (Median) gilt hat and poses him with hands forward as if holding sacred objects, but he is stark naked, which is decidedly not a feature of any Achaemenid Persian representation, but normal in Greek art [PL. XII].[168] Perhaps he once wore a dress – cloth of gold? The gold rings are 4th-century Greek (two knuckle-bone players) or Greco-Persian (addorsed bull-foreparts) in their types.[169] At Takht-I Sangin there was a gold ring with a turquoise intaglio of Greco-Persian type.[170]

In 1993 another large hoard, parts of it closely comparable to the Oxus Treasure, came to light and is largely housed in the Miho Museum in Japan.[171] Russian archaeologists, who had believed that the original Oxus Treasure represented material once at the temple at Takht-I Sangin, hailed it as part of the same treasure.[172] Some scholars have expressed strong suspicions about the authenticity of many of the objects, but to the writer most seem genuine enough. But although many of them are decidedly 'Persian' in appearance, some are later than much in the old Oxus Treasure. Moreover, it has been suggested that the new treasure is simply part of a much larger find of precious objects from Mir-Zakah in western Gandhara, to the south, including thousands of coins and objects going as late perhaps as the 1st century AD, and not from the Oxus area at all. It may really be a matter of several 'hoards' created at various times since antiquity, mainly from Mir-Zakah, one batch of which at least somewhat resembles the content of the first Oxus Treasure, although perhaps not from so far north. Whatever the truth of the matter, many of the objects of the new treasure are relevant since they are Greek or graecizing products with that eastern flavour which we have learned to expect of the Greco-Bactrian kingdoms. Of the Greek material what seem to me the most significant are the gold rings and gems. But whether any of them need to be as late as the Greco-Bactrian kingdom is another matter, and it might well be that at least this part of the find (not the majority of the coins) represents the product of a crisis of the period of the invasions; a few seem 'Hellenistic' enough to leave discussion of them in this chapter rather than any earlier.[173]

The finds include more finger rings of Greek types, but also intaglios, Greek and Greco-Persian. The jewelry is mainly Persian or eastern and there are several Persian-type bracelets and cups (phialai). More substantial are silver-gilt rhyta of Persian type, but some with realistic animal protomes reflecting the Hellenistic versions of the Seleucid and Parthian world, which include remarkable essays of modelling and imagination. Other gilt silver vessels carry more Greek decoration, including one with high-relief figures in a Dionysiac scene with maenads, musicians and the god [PL. XIV; the silver corroded black]. A silver dish with a *ketos* (sea monster) reminds us of this monster, a Greek creation with a strong eastern history.[174] Many gold plaques with figures of Persian worshippers, like those from the Oxus Treasure, are accompanied by others that are classical in dress and pose. The ill-defined history of the hoard, like so much else from the area, must not distract attention from the importance of the finds and their character, implying as they do a society well conversant with Greek manners, and indeed artists working in the pure tradition of the homeland, and apparently into the period after the fall of the Achaemenid Persian Empire.

Their coinage

A long section devoted to coinage might seem out of proportion but in our area and period coinage is important for more than study of mercenary matters. It was in everyone's hands. It demonstrated graphically who was in command, and more subtly, from the usually divine subjects of the reverses, it could comment on matters beyond the religious. Its inscriptions in the east are not all Greek and they tell us about how non-Greeks could use this gift from the west. Its art in the east could be sublime and match anything of the Greek homeland. Moreover, the evidence in the east has become plentiful, largely from hoards. Separate consideration here of the coinage is justified for two different reasons: it derives from western practices, providing a continuum which deserves to be looked at in more than passing historical comments, and it sometimes involves matters that go beyond the immediate concerns of a person or place.[175]

In the Persian period there had already been some local production of imitations of Athenian 'owl' coins, and some punch-marked oval and discoid concave coins punch-marked with various patterns, not inscriptions, barely coins at all [47].[176]

A Seleucid satrap called Sophytos, probably an Indian by birth, had started minting coins of Greek type in the early 3rd century BC,[177] and we have seen that Greek coinage, even locally produced, was no novelty for the east. But Diodotos begins the major Greco-Bactrian series, one of the most distinguished for its quality and originality in the whole Greek world.

The coinage of the Bactrian and Indo-Greek kings provides us with important, if sometimes equivocal evidence for the history of their rule. In itself it is remarkable as one of the few Greek arts to flourish for so long and in its native form so far east, in a form often purer than that of the Greek or Greek-inspired artists and architects working in the same regions. It has other things to teach, however, about symbolism and Greek iconography in the service of power politics outside the Greek and Seleucid worlds, but also, since so many of the coins were struck for a non-Greek population, about the juxtaposition of Greek and oriental subjects and language. That the kings took coinage seriously may be judged from the fact that some minted imposing coins of medallion-like size and weight, possibly mindful of their role almost as jewelry as much as for exchange, often in the hands of the non-Greek; many homeland Greeks might have thought them hybristic. The size and magnificence of much of the coinage is sometimes marred by mistakes in the inscriptions. This might suggest that non-Greek artisans played a role in the creation of the coin dies,[178] but a degree of illiteracy among Greek artists even at home is well attested (on painted vases, for example).

Punch-marked silver bars were being used in Paropamisadae (south of Bactria) even while the Achaemenid satraps still ruled there, and a few Persian coins had also passed east, although they were more plentifully current in the western empire. The punched bars give rise to the square coins of the Indian Mauryan kings from before 300 BC on, and although these were no longer made after the fall of the empire in the later 2nd century, they continued to be

47 Punch-marked silver coin from north India.
Late 4th century BC. (London, British Museum)

used for centuries. At Aï Khanoum a hoard of 677 such punch-marked coins was found with just six of the Greek King Agathokles; but the latter are bilinguals, Greek and Indian, and of Indian shape.[179] Such are the models, in form alone, for many other coins minted by the Greek kings. But we start in Bactria.

The obverses of the coins usually carry the royal portrait. Symbols of Macedonian kingship are not eschewed: the diadem band and, from the 180s on, the flat-cap *kausia*. Demetrios I adopts the elephant headdress [PL. XXIII],[180] which had been worn by Alexander on Ptolemaic coins and by successor rulers, including Seleukos I; and Eukratides I wears a fine cavalry helmet decorated with horn and ear [PL. XXIV], which might recall Alexander's 'horned' horse Bucephalus, and had appeared, on a different helmet type, for Seleukos I. Heliokles I, Menander and Amyntas dared show their busts wearing an aegis, which is more familiar to us as Athena's magic goatskin wrap, a very explicit bid for divinity, as is the *theos* ('god') in legends of coins of Agathokles and Antimachos I. The bust, three-quarter back, with the aegis, is almost a novelty even for its prime wearer, Zeus.[181] The aegis will occupy us further.

Of other epithets *soter* ('saviour') is common, even *dikaios* ('just'), while Eukratides I is 'the Great' (*megas*), or at least 'Overlord'. In their Indian legends in the Kharoshti or Brahmi scripts, each king is declared a true *maharaja*. There are a few commemorative issues. Agathokles compliments Diodotos I by repeating his head and reverse type (Zeus), where his own name appears; Antimachos I does the same for him, and for Euthydemos I; Eukratides celebrates his parents Heliokles and Laodike.

The reverses, usually showing deities, can be more informative, and our enquiry becomes as much iconographic as numismatic. Those who determined the devices for the coins were not mindless in their choices, simply copying established Hellenistic or earlier types. Several are significant variations on what we see elsewhere in the Greek world, and we should remark on them even if we cannot always explain them.

There were Bactrian gold and silver issues for the Seleucid Antiochos II, with his portrait and an Apollo reverse. Then Diodotos I mints with his own portrait, but on the reverse a Zeus, though he still names Antiochos, whom he then comes to replace with his own name. The Zeus is interesting [PL. XXV],

48 Silver coin of Menander, the reverse featuring Athena wielding a thunderbolt. Mid-2nd century BC.

a slim archaic or early classical figure flourishing a thunderbolt, long familiar. But here he has his aegis, with gorgoneion, slung from his outstretched arm like a shield, and this is odd. The aegis belonged to him before being worn by Athena, but he is seldom seen wearing it. Alexander as Zeus could adopt it, but its addition to this Zeus type seems novel, though it appears shortly afterwards in Greece (Epirus).[182] The other major striding, striking deity for Greek art is Athena with her spear, a Promachos, and the figure, on tiptoe, is a Hellenistic type, commonly related to an Athena Alkidemos which stood at Pella in Macedonia and which appears on many Hellenistic coins. For us she appears first with Menander and often thereafter [**48**], but always with the thunderbolt, and without a spear, which is the usual western type.[183] Moreover, Menander has some coins of her with the aegis on her outstretched arm as on Diodotos' Zeus, and not her usual shield. This she had not done for many years in Greek art although the archaizing type may have been known in the Hellenistic period,[184] when the aegis becomes more fashionable for divinity, as on the Great Altar at Pergamum; but our coins are special cases, especially in the east. Such iconographic details are significant. The aegis can tell a lot about coin symbolism. Archebios has a blitzing Zeus, frontal, and Heliokles I and others have him standing with the bolt.

Seated Zeus is at his best in frontal/three-quarters view from Antialkidas on, and on some coins of Amyntas and, later, Hermaios, his head is radiate. Zeus holding a Hekate on his hand [**PL. XXVI**], for Agathokles and Pantaleon, or an Athena for Amyntas, are unexpected combinations, probably reflecting various local cult associations. The relevance of the deity to the ruler is seldom particularly apparent; in landlocked Bactria a Poseidon could have more to do with earthquakes than the sea, but there are other aquatic themes. The bolt also appears alone on coins of Indian shape.[185] In favouring these attributes our Indo-Greek moneyers must have had ideas of their significance, riverine if not marine.

These figures derive, as does much else in Hellenistic coin iconography, from classical sculptural models, such as the Pheidian seated Zeus at Olympia. Other figures on the Bactrian and Indo-Greek coins have the same source but often without obvious precedent in coinage farther west. The Artemis with her torch on Diodotos' coins may also have her dog, as in the sculpture groups; for Demetrios I and others she draws an arrow in another familiar type. Given the prominence accorded to Dionysos in Greek stories about the east it is perhaps surprising to see so little of anything Dionysiac on the coins, except for his bust on coins of Agathokles and Pantaleon. The weary but triumphant Herakles seated on rocks is a traditional figure deriving from the sculptor Lysippos, but when he appears first for us, with Euthydemos I [PL. XXVII], his club is propped on a rock pillar, which seems an intimation of a different though related statuary group.[186] Crowning himself, for Demetrios I and others, he is a Hellenistic type, first here on coins.[187] His role as the hero/god paradigm for rulers is of considerable antiquity in Greek art and thought, reinforced by Alexander's use of his image. Of other heroes, the galloping Dioskouroi introduced by Eukratides I [PL. XXIV] have antecedents but are nowhere better composed for coins, and with original variations (the turned horse's head). The pair appear also standing and symbolized by their two *pilos* hats, and they have other eastern connotations (cf. ills. **46**, **148**). The same may be said for the goddess with cornucopia, probably Tyche, seated (for Amyntas on his big silver) [**49**], and standing on coins of Indian shape for Philoxenos. The debt of the iconography of the Indian goddess Hariti to such figures is generally acknowledged (see also below). The unusual type of Skylla or Triton, with fishy legs and unique in this type on coins, was adopted in the late period by Telephos [**50**],[188] and on Hippostratos' Indian coins. It too will contribute

49 Silver coin of Amyntas. On the reverse, an enthroned Tyche holds a cornucopia. 1st cent. BC.

50 Silver coin of Euergetes. On the obverse, a Triton; on the reverse, Helios and Selene (Sun and Moon) and a Kharoshti inscription. 1st cent. BC.

to the iconography of Indian 'Triton' figures and, holding oar and dolphin, as he does for Hippostratos, is recalled in the later arts of Yuehzhi Bactria, as we shall see. Helios standing, with Selene for Telephos, or in his chariot, is seen on coins of Platon; he will serve as model for the Indian sun god, Surya. Poseidon will serve as model for figures of Shiva. However, these radiate figures, Apollo, Helios or Zeus-Helios, may also be interpreted as an allusion to Mithra, the Persian deity long venerated far to the east. This is most convincing where the Zeus wears a 'Mithraic cap', conical with a nodding crown (coins of Hermaios; and later worn by some Kushan kings). The only problem here is that Artemis too may appear radiate on a type with an otherwise impeccable Hellenistic sculptural pedigree.[189] This radiance seems another eastern characteristic.

The range of devices on the coins of Indian shape (square) and other bilinguals makes few concessions to the experience of those expected to handle them. Many of these coins are of copper (or nickel). Most carry the royal portraits and a range of the other Greek devices seen on the principal Greek-inscribed silver issues. Only Agathokles and Pantaleon, with the earliest of these and in their Taxila mint, make a point of showing Indian deities, as well as symbols (the stylized mountain – Meru? – and the sacred tree in an enclosure) which appear on native Indian coins;[190] while Menander shows the eastern *chakra*, wheel of destiny. Appropriate animal devices include the elephant, zebu bull, and standing lion, the last more Persian or Indian than Greek, although it appears in Greek style with a raised paw for Menander II. Otherwise Greek subjects are recruited – club, wreath, aegis, thunderbolt, dolphin, cornucopia, tripod, bucranium, boar's head, etc. – although not all of them used on the larger silver. Apollodotos II resurrects the old seated Apollo testing his arrow who had served as model for many Persian and Hellenistic devices, including Seleucid.

Stylistically the Bactrian and Indo-Greek series must be judged as being as well composed and executed as most in the Hellenistic world, while their iconographic range, even apart from the Indian devices, is more varied than most. Only with Hermaios do we begin to detect a retreat into pattern for the treatment of heads and bodies rather than even summary treatment of classical and at least semi-realistic forms.

And their legacy? 'Hermaios' coins go on being minted after his death, in an increasingly debased form, even until the first of the Kushan kings.[191] The coins of the Scythian kings take their lead from the Greek, but without the portrait heads: instead, the king is seated cross-legged, or is a horseman, sometimes in armour. The other devices are simply copied from the Greek – Zeus, Tyche, Athena, Nike, the Dioskouroi, the rest – but even here we may find innovations as yet not traced to their sources. Thus, we have for King Azes a Poseidon in the usual classical pose but accompanied by a reclining river god,[192] while Maues has him thus also holding a thunderbolt. These are unique combinations for the god in or outside the Greek world, and it is as though the Indo-Greek Poseidon had become obliged to share the limelight with a major river (the Indus?) and had usurped Zeus' thunderbolt for the occasion.[193] These images could only have been composed, and executed, by a Greek. Imitation of anything remotely Roman is vestigial or highly dubious.[194]

Parthian coins minted for India follow suit, but some carry Parthian portrait heads and figures. Parthian coinage remotely reflects Greek precedent, with the royal heads, but debased versions styled more directly on the Greek appear; one, for example, with a garbled version of a Parthian royal head on one side [51], and a version of the seated king with his bow, which had graced Persian [15] and Seleucid issues.[195]

The earliest Kushan coins roughly follow suit, but the range of mainly standing deities on the later Kushan coins of India has many sources, among which the Greek are still prominent beside some Roman, but already subject to many local transformations and in an Indian style that remains quite distinct from the classical western.[196]

51 Silver Parthian coin from Bokhara. The reverse has a debased version of the older Greek motif of a king seated testing his arrow. (After *DCAA*)

CHAPTER 5
Greeks and their arts in Central Asia

Greeks and nomads: Scythians, Sarmatians

At this point my narrative is less about Greek presence in Asia than about the effect of Greeks and their arts in Asia; more archaeological-cum-art-historical than straight history, and much is more northerly. We have had to consider in the last chapter, beside excavated and datable works, much that is from undated hoards or uncertain excavated contexts. This material covers the period immediately subsequent to Alexander's conquest. There is much more besides, especially in south Central Asia, which displays Greek influence and perhaps workmanship in what appears to be the same period – not strictly either Bactrian Greek or Indo-Greek, but highly expressive of Greek presence from the Hellenistic period on, quite apart from what was happening in Parthia, to which we shall return, or from what had happened earlier, out of the Black Sea area to the north. We are dealing with a period in which cross-continental routes are opening up yet more vigorously. That 'European Scythians' and 'Asian Scythians' may need distinguishing, but can be considered as a single continuum, is a fair indication of the geographical problems.[197] The Scythians, or Saka as they are known in Central Asia, are in touch with Greek behaviour around the Black Sea and from south of the Caucasus. Meanwhile there are major states developing among the greater cities like Bokhara, Samarkand and Tashkent. Movement from the east, from the Altai Mountains of Siberia, and around the Taklamakan desert from China's borders, is strongly in evidence. The Persian legacy is evident still too in Siberia (the Altai) and Bactria. The Greeks are not prime movers in this, but, being Greeks and given the apparently influential aspects of their arts – both narrative and naturalistic, and already not a little redolent of eastern practices – their effects are manifest. And from the 3rd century on they are in residence in some numbers, not just along the Oxus in Bactria, but, it seems, to the north where the Scythians and Sarmatians ruled, and east (Ferghana) towards China and the peoples on Chinese frontiers. Evidence is generally scattered and seldom usefully centres on a single site.

Distinguishing Scythians and Sarmatians (Sauromatai to Herodotus) is not easy, and perhaps not too necessary for an understanding of Central Asian affairs. They were related Indo-European nomad peoples and it is the Scythians that deal with Greeks in the north and around the Black Sea, later replaced by their kin the Sarmatians, whose arts we associate rather with later periods, and, physically, more with colourful inlaid goldwork than with the essential steppe 'Animal Style'. But it was Scythians too who had passed south of the Caspian, through Media, in the 8th/7th century BC, and left traces of steppe art in the Near East (the Ziwiye hoard),[198] and the Saka are well represented farther east, in the Ferghana area, both from finds and texts (Chinese). Herodotus' distinction between Scythians and Sarmatians helps us little, but for him the latter seem to give their women a more prominent role, a feature of much in Asian nomad culture. He gives a very full account of Scythian ways, often mistrusted by scholars of Greek history and historical texts, but very fully supported by the account of nomads offered by archaeology and Chinese historians.[199] We ignore or mistrust Herodotus at our peril.[200]

And it not only a matter of Scythians and Sarmatians. The nomads east of the Black Sea were more varied. Thus, Chorasmia, east of the Caspian, reveals different touches of Greekness on objects that are very broadly realistic and apparently pre-Alexander.

Any tidiness that might be attempted in this section must owe more to the types, objects or subjects described than to geography, and the Greekness may be diluted in various ways, yet it is often dominant. Finds range from beside the Black Sea to Kazakhstan. Thus, gold and silver medallions adopt various functions; some form part of women's jewelry, some hang on harness for horses or decorate armour (*phalera*), others decorate bowls. Two such seem typical of hellenizing Central Asia, but especially in the north; both are from Novouzensk, 275 miles (440 km) north of the Caspian. One bears a purely Greek griffin, but unnaturally elongated to fill the circle [52].[201] The other has a more informative scene of a war elephant [53], with mahout and a turreted

52 Silver gilt *phaleron* with a stretched griffin, from Novouzensk. (St Petersburg, Hermitage Museum)

53 Silver gilt *phaleron* from Novouzensk, featuring a war elephant with turreted howdah and a *ketos* on the saddle cloth. (St Petersburg, Hermitage Museum)

54 Silver gilt medallion from south Russia, with a bust of Artemis. (St Petersburg, Hermitage Museum)

howdah bearing two warriors, one wearing a Macedonian helmet, suggesting a more southerly origin for the type:[202] very Indian, at first sight, but it seems that adding a mini-fortress to an elephant's back was a Greek invention, so this is a successor to those elephants with which Indian kings used to bribe westerners. The cloth below the howdah is decorated with a Greek sea monster (*ketos*), a creature which we shall meet again and which proves to have been very influential in the east, more so than in the west where its main role as a mount for sea deities was only varied when it was adopted by artists to represent Jonah's whale.[203] A silver medallion from much farther east and probably then more like a record of Greek infiltration of northern nomad societies, like the Scythians, bears a purely Greek frontal bust of their virgin huntress goddess Artemis, slightly wild-eyed [**54**].[204] And another gilt silver goddess, winged and clutching a pomegranate, clearly betrays her classical origins but has an eastern identity (Khvaninda?). Several carry aggressively Hellenistic motifs, like a pair with Bellerophon and the Chimaera from a Sarmatian burial in west Kazakhstan [**55**].[205] At the end of the series, into years AD, Greek motifs are not forgotten but rendered in a somewhat bizarre style – strangest, perhaps, one from the Kuban with Dionysos holding a thyrsos, on a lion's back, and Athena attacking a naked, snake-wrapped, giant [**56**].[206] Truly Sarmatian *phalera* have a good range of steppe motifs, but related is a silver lid from the Astrakhan area decorated with fine incised fish and winged *ketea*, and with a very pure Greek hatched double meander [**57**].[207]

55 Silver gilt *phaleron* from Volodarka Kurgan, Kazakhstan. Bellerophon on Pegasus rides down the Chimaera. (After Mordvintseva)

56 Silver gilt *phaleron* from the Kuban. Dionysos rides a lion, and Athena fights a naked giant within a vine border. (After Mordvintseva)

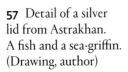

57 Detail of a silver lid from Astrakhan. A fish and a sea-griffin. (Drawing, author)

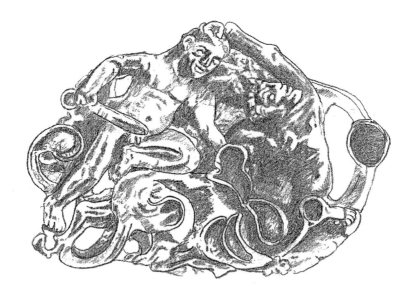

58 Gold belt plaque with inlays; a hero attacks a centaur. (Drawing, author)

The confrontation of the classical and the 'Animal Style' deserves a little digression. The Animal Style[208] had little or nothing to do with the human figure, and animal forms are stylized more conceptually than, say, the Mesopotamian, yet with close observation, and the twisting engaged figures seem as much the view from horseback of struggles on the ground as mere invention of engaging interlocking compositions. The arts of the Greeks could barely compromise with this, as we have seen, but their griffin, their own orientalizing version of the eastern monster, made its way in areas where it was said to have lived – compare the Arimasp story and our ill. **4**, and the stretched form on ill. **52**. And it continues long to appear on Central Asian artifacts, often as a Greek heraldic pair and beside patterns of a more eastern cast. Like the *ketos*, it was wholeheartedly adopted in Asia.[209]

Farther off towards China, the rich finds of the Altai and their kin, even those to the west, attest styles in bronzework which owe much to east and west but do not betray much of certain Greek inspiration.[210] There are just stray finds that suggest Greek style and subject could sometimes serve local storytelling. Plaques and hooks for belts are a major field. One isolated piece of inlaid gold [**58**][211] takes the form of a belt-hook, with a knob on its semicircular finial, a type known elsewhere in Asia and related to the more angular Parthian plaques. This has a hero attacking a centaur, a classical subject and in a classical composition, but with the expected colour inlays and a certain fluidity in parts of the body. But the hero is no ordinary Greek, nor certainly Herakles, although the group assuredly derives from western art, and the piece, with no certain provenience, is not easily assigned to any one of the various other demonstrations of Greek motifs in Asia, nor readily dated. The centaur has an odd history in the east: a very Greek version apparently dancing in a floral setting appears on a pair of 1st-century BC trousers from Sampula, in the Tarim Basin,[212] and we shall meet others.

The Yuehzhi and Tillya Tepe

We move later now, still in Central Asia on the Oxus and still with a once-nomad people, but on the brink of important new developments far to the south – the creation of the Kushan dynasty in India. And we depend almost wholly on the evidence of a single site.

The story begins in China, on its northern borders, attacked from earliest times by nomad peoples of the north and west. The most prominent of these were the Xiongnu (Hsiungnu), whose homes were in the eastern Siberian steppes. Beside them were their rivals, the Yuehzhi, an Indo-European race, nomad by origin but also more seriously horse-riding, and operating mainly from desert areas at the eastern end of the Tienshan Mountains, mainly south and west of the Xiongnu. The latter eventually attacked them and, in the early 2nd century BC, defeated them. As a result the Yuehzhi moved away, some along more southerly routes long familiar to them around the Taklamakan desert, others to the north of the Tienshan, where they met and defeated Saka/Scythians (from the Issyk-kul sites), were attacked by the probably related Wusun, and moved on through Ferghana (where Greeks lived too) to the lands north of the River Oxus.[213]

China and a Chinese now take an important role in our story. In 138 BC the Han emperor Wuti sent an envoy, Changkien, to talk to the Yuehzhi and enlist their aid against the Xiongnu.[214] He (and his embassy of 100 men) visited

Ferghana where he noted some seventy walled towns, many of them probably Greek settlements such as Alexander had founded by walling villages; hardly a Greek realm of a 'thousand cities' (Justinus 41.1), but on the way. He was captured, imprisoned, but eventually resumed his mission and met the Yuehzhi between Samarkand and the Oxus. He records their defeat of the Tahsia – the Greeks of Bactria, who were not, he remarks, a very warlike people, and who lived in walled towns and were much given to trade. This sounds totally Greek, decidedly not Macedonian – they did not want a nomad life and were only warlike when they had to be. In Ferghana and Bactria they sought a quieter existence, most like home, far from their rather more belligerent 'royal' kin to the south, and were busy traders, as ever.

The Yuehzhi went on to found the great Kushan dynasty in north India, which was soon to become Buddhist and will occupy us below.[215] Two centuries after their removal of the Greeks the Yuehzhi were still occupying Bactria, and in the 1980s Russian archaeologists excavated the burial places of one of their princes at Tillya Tepe, some 60 miles (100 km) west of Balkh/Bactra. The finds were brilliantly published by Victor Sarianidi (*TT*). Just how 'nomad' the Yuehzhi were by this time is anyone's guess; possibly very little. The burials were hugger-mugger: that is, although the bodies were quite well preserved with all their lavish dress and equipment in position, they were in rough wooden coffins and it seems likely that they had been removed from their original intended burial place, probably on the occupation site of Emshi Tepe (which might then be judged a real Yuehzhi 'township'), to be buried more safely on the older, religious site of Tillya Tepe. Coins date the burials to the mid-1st century AD.[216] They are brilliant records of a people, once nomad, with connections east to China, south to Greeks, and in an area still permeated by the traditions of Achaemenid Persian, Macedonian and Greek rule. If only archaeologists were always so lucky; without these finds our picture of Bactrian life at the dawn of the Buddhist era would have been more than sketchy and we would have been denied vivid testimony to Bactria's past.

There was one male, probably a prince, with five regal women, consorts, no doubt, and perhaps killed for the princely burial, following a familiar Asian practice. (Another burial was looted.) The clothes and grave goods were lavish, rich with gold, and for the most part, it seems, locally produced since there is great congruity of technique, if not always of style and subject, and the contents of these burials reflect in considerable detail the history of both the Yuehzhi and of the land in which they had now settled, with its rich steppe, Persian, Macedonian and Greek past. They seem to demonstrate that, whatever changes there might be in ruling classes, the people, peasants as well as merchants, craftsmen and many of the other well-to-do, still exercised a considerable influence on ways of life and art. Here we are concerned with what there is of Greeks and Greek art still apparent in the products of an ex-nomad people becoming empire-builders, but there is much too at Tillya Tepe to recall directly China and its arts, from the Yuehzhi's long period of neighbourhood and hostility to China, as well as those of the steppes and the Saka, even of Persia.

One of the women (burial 6; [60]) was most richly decked out with golden objects of Greek inspiration, perfume flasks from the Mediterranean, as well as a Chinese mirror. She held a unique gold Parthian coin in her hand, inscribed in Greek, and in her mouth a silver one with a Greek inscription (30s BC), counterstruck with the head of an Indo-Greek king.[217] The coins in hand and mouth are the Greek custom of providing for the ferryman of the dead, 'Charon's fee'.[218] The woman had been brought up as an Asian, her head deliberately deformed at birth, but intermarriage had been commonplace and there were Saka kings in the south with children bearing Greek names. One cannot but think that the lady of burial 6, and/or the women who saw to her laying-out, were in some respect conscious of and proud of some aspects of Greek heritage.

Her jewelry is the most informative, most carefully hammered from matrices and lavishly decorated with inlays of turquoise, carnelian and other precious stones or glass, in the manner we associate most with the Sarmatians of the steppes. Her gold floral crown has most to do with the steppes or even China. Her earrings were winged Erotes. Hanging from her crown were two pendants (5.8 × 4.6 cm) showing a near-naked frontal Aphrodite of Hellenistic type, flanked by two fishy monsters whose closest kin are to be found in the *makara* of north India [59].[219] Over her breasts were gold spangles including a tiny (5 cm) naked winged Aphrodite, legs swathed and leaning on a column [PL. XXXV],[220] and with a forehead 'caste mark' – an Asian sign of status. Her gold finger ring held a garnet cut with the head of a young Apollo. Among much else of varying steppe or Hellenistic style are also a millefiori glass flask and one of pale blue, of Mediterranean origin.

The most spectacular of the jewelry was hung at her neck: two clasps (7 × 6.5 cm) showing mirror images of Dionysos and Ariadne seated on the

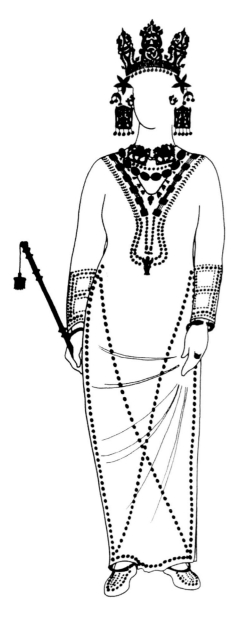

59 ABOVE Gold plaque from Tillya Tepe with Aphrodite and monsters. 1st cent. AD. (Drawing, author. After *TTG*)

60 LEFT The woman from burial 6 at Tillya Tepe. For the ornaments at ears and neck, see **PLS. XXXII** and **XXXI**. (After *TT*)

back of a lion that sports a griffin's mane and some leaf-like excrescences (acanthoid) [**PL. XXXI**],[221] a Hellenistic feature exploited in various ways in the east. The god holds a cup poised over the horn-cup of a kneeling satyr who is dressed in his belted hairy pelt (rather than growing it, as he should). The pair are being crowned by Victory/Nike and their dress is as it would have been in Greece but for the thick sleeves and cap of Ariadne – these are nomad dress. The Nike shows that this is more than a wedding and that it must owe something to classical scenes of the Triumph of Dionysos over the Indians, a subject gaining a new lease of life once celebration of the comparable Triumph of Alexander in the east had adopted the theme also, assimilating mortal to god, an easy process in this case. If so, it is the single direct reference in art in the east to the Triumph of Dionysos,[222] and would have been much in the traditions of the Indo-Greeks, whatever their views about Alexander/Dionysos and the Macedonians.

Burial 6 had the lion's share of the hellenizing material, but there is no little in the other graves which is closely comparable, for instance another naked, winged Aphrodite standing between two columns, and now with an Eros at her shoulder, but she is wearing what looks most like a Persian cap [**PL. XXXIV**].[223] There are Greek and Greco-Persian engraved gems, inscribed in Greek, some from earlier periods; and splendid roundels and hair-pins combining Greek acanthus with eastern lotus [**PL. XXXIII**].[224] There are several more Erotes, riding dolphins or alone. Two larger plaques [**PL. XXXII**],[225] mirror images, have a burly warrior in hellenizing armour, in what looks like a monster arbour (with winged lions), and with features that no little resemble those of Alexander, whose image was well known in the east.[226] The warrior prince's own belt was of eastern type, of connected discs, each showing a woman holding a drinking cup of Greek shape (often found in the east) and riding a lion [61].[227] Nanaia/Nana was an eastern lion-rider, from Mesopotamia to India,[228] but not with a cup, and she could be assimilated to Athena or Artemis; this one is more like a Greek maenad, of which there is the earlier Greco/Scythian example from near the Black Sea, where her dress is Greek but with thick steppe sleeves [6], as also worn by our Ariadne.[229] So this looks like another assimilation of a Greek figure to an eastern one. Finally, a series of plaques shows a fish-legged figure,

61 Inlaid gold roundel from a belt. A goddess (eastern maenad?) seated on a lion and holding a cup. 1st cent. AD. (Drawing, author. After *TTG*)

62 Inlaid gold plaque with a Triton holding an oar and a dolphin. 1st cent. AD. (Drawing, author. After *TTG*)

with acanthus skirt [62],[230] just like a Greek Triton, carrying an oar and with a dolphin wrapped around his neck. All the elements of the Greek Triton are there though they are never (it seems) so combined in the west, but the figure recurs in the east, on an Indo-Greek coin (of Hippostratos), a gem, a relief and a palette [91],[231] while a Kushan coin [63] has a male holding a dolphin and labelled OAXO, so there are good reasons to think that it may represent the River Oxus itself.

63 Design of a man holding a dolphin from a Kushan silver coin. 1st cent. AD. (Drawing, author. After *TTG*)

The whole complex can be seen to be rather like that at Begram, which we have yet to consider, with the profound difference that at Begram the range of foreign goods and associations was demonstrated by many imported objects, mainly of later date, but at Tillya Tepe largely by precious objects made locally and strongly reflecting a very similar range of influences.

The farther east

The Greeks in Central Asia were dealing with many peoples whose homes had been farther to the east, notably the Yuehzhi who had fought the Chinese on their northeastern border, and they were themselves observed and commented on by the Chinese envoy. Alexander may have intended to take his armies farther east, but only in India, and an Indo-Greek king did indeed raid far along the Ganges to Pataliputra. Of other direct and deliberate Greek interests in the direction of China we hear and see nothing, yet there are strange echoes of Greekness, and with the Christian era, clear indications of trade interests, often of Roman goods (glass) into Chinese lands.

A feature of the Chinese/nomad struggles of the last centuries BC (mainly 5th to 2nd) was, in archaeological terms, the use of decorated belt plaques of styles which lend themselves readily to stylistic classification and historical associations.[232] Overall the designs are Chinese or strongly reminiscent of the steppe styles of nomads, even Scythians, although quite distinct from them in their farther eastern manifestations. Among them I have found one pair of 4th-century gold plaques [**PL. XXIII**] in a puzzling style that had nothing in common with the rest, though the subject is as one might expect, and they were clearly made in north China – inscribed on the back with their weight and a description ('tiger and pig').[233] The fine incised decoration has more in common with the sub-archaic styles of Asia Minor in Persian times – 5th/4th centuries BC – than with anything else (compare ill. **8**). There is Persian influence in the Altai; that a Greco-Persian could have gone farther east is by no means inconceivable.

A different indication of awareness of the Greek west is purely iconographic and concerns the appearance of the Greek sea monster (*ketos*), whose varied fortunes in Central Asia and India occupy us more than once in this book.[234] The relevant feature is its head, with a long snout, bridged nose, pointed ears and often horns, beard, and leafy (acanthoid) excrescences. These all become features of the Chinese dragon as it begins to be depicted in the early Han period (2nd/1st centuries BC). Before, their dragon had been rather fish-like or feline; now it is reptilian with clawed feet, but its head appears suddenly quite transformed and more like that of the Greek *ketos* than anything that had appeared before in Chinese or Asian art [**64**]. Given its success in Central Asia and India it is perhaps not surprising that it should have been noticed also by Chinese artists, and with long-lasting effects.[235]

Otherwise there is a scatter of finds that indicate how far objects can travel and sometimes the unexpected influence they might have on local craftsmen.

64 *Ketos* and dragon heads. Left – Chinese; right – Greek; below – Tillya Tepe. (Drawing, author. After *After Alexander*)

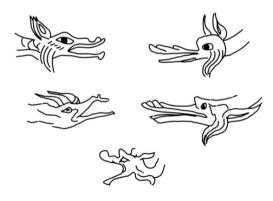

65 Gilt bronze cup from Datong (Shanxi, China) with a Vintage scene. 1st/2nd cent. AD (?). (After Rawson)

For the objects, there is an early Roman *gryllos* gem in south Indo-China, a lamp in Thailand and glass in Korea.[236] In south Thailand a bronze bowl from a site mainly of the 4th to 2nd century BC (Khao Sam Kaeo) has a whirl of rows of animals including an unmistakable griffin.[237] There is Greek 'black-glazed' pottery from north Malaya (Perlis).[238] In China a lobed cup with animals added atop derives from a Greco-Persian heritage,[239] and from Datong (Shanxi) is a gilt bronze cup with a vintage scene which is wholly classical, probably of the early centuries AD [65].[240] From Jingyuan (Gansu) comes a gilt silver plate showing Dionysos on a leopard in a heavy vine border and marked with a Greek/Bactrian weight inscription, probably dating to the 1st century BC/ AD [66].[241] A Chinese bronze sword handle carries felines related to those on belt plaques but also a facing horned, eared, bearded, mask very like a satyr's of earlier date.[242] More remarkable is the Sasanian-type silver gilt flask found in the tomb of a Chinese general (Li Xian; died AD 569) in north China with

66 Gilt silver plate from Jingyuan (Gansu, China), featuring Dionysos on a leopard within a vineyard border. 1st/2nd cent. AD. (After *China Digest*)

what seem to be extracts from scenes of the Trojan epics.[243] Farther off, there are elements in Japanese arts, deriving mainly via China, that attest distant classical influence, mainly the use of vinous motifs, and these persist for long in their new environment, with masks that might ultimately derive from oriental translations of a gorgoneion.[244]

Eastwards, the route up from Gandhara towards the passes into China (at Gilgit) yields a native version of a Greek centaur-rhyton in bronze [**PL. XXX**],[245] and at the other end of the Taklamakan desert along the Silk Road a kneeling bronze warrior combines Greek with Phrygian (the helmet) and is said to be from a 4th-century BC grave [**67**].[246] So far from home it is later periods that reveal continuity of use of classical motifs – some architectural, some iconographic, like the flying women with blown dress, floral swags and rinceaux, realistic body-modelling and shading – mainly too distant in time and place, from the Taklamakan desert to China, to attest any direct contact with their ultimate western sources.[247] For much of this we are indebted to the discoveries of explorers of more than a century ago – Sir Aurel Stein, Albert von Le Coq and others.

From the Chinese point of view any westerners were only of immediate importance if they could be useful or if they fostered trade, principally in silk,[248] but trade was conducted hand-to-hand and it takes some time before China seems to have any serious knowledge of what lay beyond Central Asia and its populations – of whom they were well aware having to fight them so often. We have seen how an embassy went west in the reign of the emperor Wuti (141–87 BC) to consult the Yuehzhi, observing Greeks to the south as well as making mention of India (Shentu) and Parthia (Anhsi). They returned in 114 BC with much information, and specimens of flora and fauna. In AD 97 there was an embassy (led by Gan Ying) to the Tach'in, probably not the Romans but peoples of the west Persian Gulf (Tiaochih = Tigris?), while the Parthians and Indians were sending embassies and gifts

67 Bronze kneeling warrior from a burial north of the Tienshan range. (Urumchi Museum. After *DCAA*. H. 42 cm)

to the Han court. Antioch (Charax) at the Tigris mouth may have been the principal port of contact, carrying goods from the Greek and Roman world arriving via Palmyra to proceed by sea, not land, to the east, and so a major source for Mediterranean trade with India beside that via the Red Sea.[249] The Emperor Claudius (reigned AD 41–54) sent an embassy to Sri Lanka (Pliny, *Nat. Hist.* 6.24) but trade with the Chinese was never to be a simple face-to-face affair rather than stage by stage along the silk roads (ibid., 6.54).[250]

There is a very classical Chinese riding down a boar on an exquisite but quite undatable gold buckle from a site in Tajikistan [**PL. XXIX**],[251] but there is a further possible trace of classical influence in China which has been discussed recently, although I am uncertain about its true relevance. Chinese art is most notable for its exquisite essays in stylization of natural forms. However, the First Emperor (died 207 BC), with his 'terracotta army', offers a degree of realism and individuality in the treatment of human physique and features that is quite at variance with this tradition. It has been suggested[252] that this is the result of knowledge of classical realism, which we cannot trace in execution farther east than the Taklamakan desert. Moreover, the emperor set up a series of twelve colossal bronze statues which, it is suggested, were inspired by the Twelve God statues said to have been erected by Alexander the Great's army at the confines of India before they turned for home.[253] But those are attested only by Diodorus Siculus at a time when the mythologization of Alexander was already well established, and it is not an act which matches Alexander's other, better attested bids for fame – the naming of cities and probably erection of statues to himself and family.

The Chinese figures are a matter of appearance, not technique. But the appeal of 'realism' could be experienced by any artist at any time and without contact with other realists. It may be a rare phenomenon, but it happened even in Central America, otherwise totally committed to extreme stylization and out of touch with 'classicism', and far earlier in many palaeolithic cave paintings. The fashion did not linger in China, and when in the 1st century BC Han painters came close to very realistic rendering of human forms and dress, it was without in any way betraying anything 'classical'. That arrived only with Buddhist arts from India, much later.[254]

XIV Gilt silver cup with maenads, one naked playing a *syrinx*, another dressed, with a torch. 3rd/2nd cent. BC. (Miho Museum, Shigaraki. H. 13.2 cm)

XV, **XVI** Reconstructions of the city at Aï Khanoum. ABOVE Courtyard with entrances to iwans. BELOW The city and fortifications alongside the river. (After Bernard)

XVII Gilt silver disc from Aï Khanoum, showing the goddess Cybele in a chariot, with priests, a radiate bust of a god, the moon and sun. 3rd cent. BC. (After *Afghanistan*. Diam. 24 cm)

XVIII Bronze statuette of a piping satyr, dedicated at Takht-I Sangin by one Atrosokes. 3rd cent. BC. (After *Oxus*. H. 33 cm)

XIX Ivory scabbard from Takht-I Sangin with a lion holding a deer, and on the chape a curled-up goat in nomad style. 4th cent. BC. (After *Oxus*. L. 27.7 cm)

XX Ivory forepart of a rhyton vase in the form of a lion, from Takht-I Sangin. 4th/3rd cent. BC. (After *Oxus*. H. 8.6 cm)

XXI Ivory head of Herakles wearing a lionskin cap, the pelt over his shoulders, from Takht-I Sangin. 3rd cent. BC. (After *Oxus*. Height 3.6 cm)

XXII Ivory relief from a scabbard with a winged female horse-fish, holding an oar and fruit, from Takht-I Sangin. 3rd cent. BC. (After *Oxus*. Width 11.8 cm)

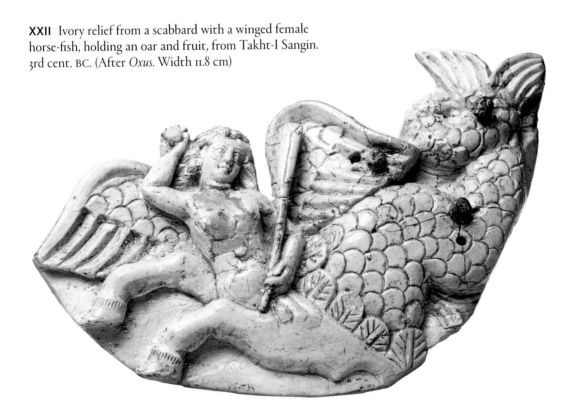

XXIII TOP LEFT Coin of
Demetrios I wearing an
elephant head as headdress.
Early 2nd cent. BC.

XXIV TOP RIGHT Coin of
Eukratides I wearing a cavalry
helmet. On the reverse, the
Dioskouroi on horses.
2nd cent. BC.

XXV ABOVE LEFT Coin of
Diodotos I. On the reverse
Zeus striding forward, his aegis
draped over his arm and raising
a thunderbolt. 3rd cent. BC.

XXVI ABOVE CENTRE Coin
of Agathokles. On the reverse
Zeus with a sceptre and holding
a small figure of the goddess
Hekate. Early 2nd cent. BC.

XXVII ABOVE RIGHT Coin of
Euthydemos. On the reverse
Herakles with his club seated
on rocks. Late 3rd cent. BC.

XXIII TOP Gold belt plaque showing a lion and boar fighting, in an unusual and possibly western style. From Xigoupan, north China. 5th/4th cent. BC (?) (After Boardman. 13 × 10 cm)

XXIX ABOVE Gold belt buckle from Tajikistan. A Chinese horseman rides down a boar. The border is a classical ovolo. (After *Treasures*. W. 5.2 cm)

XXX Bronze rhyton in the form of a centaur holding a goat, from near Gilgit, Pakistan. 3rd/2nd century BC. (Oxford, Ashmolean Museum 1963.28. H. 27.5 cm)

CHAPTER 6
Greeks and their arts in India

'India' for our purposes includes modern Pakistan, all the Indus Valley up to the mountain barrier before China, as well as much that is now east Afghanistan. Here we meet Buddhism, the most conspicuous religion considered in this book, apart from the 'classical' where our interest has been mainly iconographic.

Alexander had to face, and defeat, an Indian king, Poros, and there have been occasions already to notice Indian connexions – as at Aï Khanoum, while even in the Bronze Age there had been clear contacts between the Indus Valley civilizations and the Oxus, even with Mesopotamia.[255] After Alexander, the first major indications of Greek influence and presence involve firstly the Mauryan dynasty (321–180 BC) and developing Buddhism, largely in the north, and secondly the Sunga dynasty (185–75 BC), which succeeds the Mauryan, and demonstrates a quite different character, mainly in north India itself (the Ganges Valley and farther south). Thirdly we revert farther to the north, from the Mauryans on, notably in Gandhara, with the continuing Greek presence, as at the city of Taxila, resulting in a strong classical influence on Buddhist art which continued uninterrupted into centuries AD under the Kushans.

The evidence will prove largely archaeological but here it is appropriate to discuss the few literary sources.[256] For our period there is little of historical importance in India, beyond the record in the *Milindapahna* of the Greek King Menander's discussions with the Buddhist sage Nagasena. But there are several Greek sources, even apart from the historians whose interest was largely in Alexander. In the early 3rd century BC Seleukos I sent to the court of Chandragupta, whom we shall soon meet, the Greek Megasthenes, on the first of several missions, resulting in a history (*Indika*) in four volumes.[257] He spent most of his time in Pataliputra, far to the east, and describes the country and its people as an ethnographer rather than a historian, with no little interest in mythography and its connections with the Hellenic, notably Herakles

(= Shiva) and Dionysos (= Krishna or Indra). Of his text too little is preserved but he spent most of his time in the east, quite far from areas most pervaded by Greeks and Greekness, though not altogether immune to them, especially in architecture, as we shall see.

In the 1st century AD Apollonios of Tyana (in Cappadocia), a wandering philosopher/sage, visited India and Taxila and spoke with their wise men, according to his biographer Philostratos (two centuries later).[258] India was always going to be a great resource for tales of the mysterious: such as the giant Indian ants (really marmots) who dug for gold and might be related to the fossil dragons of north India recorded by later Greeks.[259] Later, the neo-Platonists and early Christians, notably those from Syria and Alexandria, were to take an interest in the Brahmans and the Buddha. But India had never been a total mystery to Greeks, from early classical times on.[260]

In this chapter we shall also be addressing Buddhist art, mainly for the contribution made to it by classicizing subjects and style – but it developed its own styles and narrative which owed less to the west.[261]

The Mauryans and Buddhism

Although the Mauryan dynasty had centred on the Ganges Valley, its rule and activity extended well to the north, into Gandhara and areas permeated by Greeks. Its first king was well known to the Greeks as Sandracotta (Chandragupta) – and according to Indian sources he had been assisted to power by Greeks ('Yavana'). Its third king Asoka (reigned 268–232 BC) converted to Buddhism and this occasioned the creation of new monuments of architectural and sculptural importance. The 'stupas' are a major source: domed structures meant to house relics of the Buddha and surrounded by a walkway with monumental gates and steps lavishly adorned with relief sculpture, highly colourful originally. We shall learn more about the Buddhist stupa shrines with the Sunga dynasty, but Asoka especially celebrated his reign by the erection of single stone pillars on which his edicts were inscribed, placed all across north India; his maxims, some hold, were not without the influence of those of Greek origin, such as were displayed at Aï Khanoum.[262] We

68 Stone capital from Rampurva. A zebu bull; lotus and palmette on the plinth. 3rd cent. BC. (After *DCAA*)

have already noted his bilingual rock inscription at Kandahar. The pillars are crowned by baluster capitals which may look somewhat Achaemenid (like Persian bases) but are more probably a translation into stone of wooden pillars with cushion tops designed to support tentage, and they are well endowed with varieties of Greek floral friezes.[263] But they are also crowned by sculptures of a type without Indian precedent. A zebu bull is an eastern creature but here (on the Rampurva pillar) carved realistically [**68**].[264] The Sarnath pillar top (now the Indian national symbol) [**PL. XXXVII**][265] is crowned by three seated lions whose semi-realism and box-like muzzles have more Hellenistic/Persian about them than anything in preceding local art, and the relief animals in panels beneath them are pure Greek in style, while the relief friezes of lotus and flame-palmettes could hardly be more Hellenistic. It was perhaps these pillars that Strabo (3.5.6) or Apollodoros (3.5.2) found attributed to Dionysos or Herakles, and allegedly inscribed with their deeds.

The Sunga dynasty

The Sunga dynasty (185–75 BC) was centred more in north India proper, along the Ganges Valley and to the south, although it was essentially also the successor to the Mauryans. However, the Greek elements of the Mauryan heritage in the arts are best pursued in the north, in Gandhara, into centuries AD, and are considered below, while under the Sunga quite different influences from the same quarter produced quite different results. These are more architectural in content, while in sculpture they resemble most the Achaemenid response to Greek arts, by being selective of motifs and patterns. In these respects they presage less the 'Gandhara style' than does the record in the north.

The principal sites are major stupas at Sanchi and Bharhut, with a sculptural school also at Mathura, and far to the east at Pataliputra, a site that has yielded important architectural elements. We may recall that Indo-Greek kings, like Demetrios and perhaps Menander, were bold enough to penetrate that far east with force of arms but to no significant effect that we can detect.

Precedent styles of figure art in north India had been varied, more often in terracotta, often rather fussily decorative and their treatment of the human, especially female, form had always expressed that distinctive appreciation of the rotund, which was less evident in the hellenizing arts though certainly not absent. Now it is expressed in new postures and compositions which are broadly classical, with contrapposto and back views, and a new interest in free-standing figures. On the stupas the small reliefs betray the west more in simple iconographic details, like the flying figures with garlands, which are the eastern kin of classical Victories, or groups like a frontal chariot of the sun god.

For single monumental figures the influence is more selective and strongly resembles the approach of Achaemenid sculptors some four centuries earlier, introducing overlapping folds of dress on to what was otherwise foldless: in Greek terms almost more archaic than classical. An exaggerated example of the motif appears on a figure from Bharhut [69], for what looks like an Indian rendering of a foreign figure with a long Asian sword.[266] It seems more natural on a free-standing figure from Vidisa.[267] On reliefs the hovering *apsaras* in pairs, with flying dress, take the form of a Greek Nike/Victory, as seen in many an arch corner, and as on our **PL. XXXI**. In India too they may

69 Relief of a warrior with long sword and archaizing classical dress, from Bharhut. 1st cent. BC. (Calcutta Museum. After *DCAA*)

70 In this relief from Bharhut, winged apsaras attend a stupa. 1st cent. BC. (Calcutta Museum.)

carry wreaths [**70**],[268] and the motif will have a very long history in eastern Asia.[269] Following this comes a more realistic treatment of the otherwise lush body forms so familiar in Indian art for centuries to come, a manner which begins in Sanchi with figures more voluptuous even than the Hellenistic, if sometimes less anatomically plausible (a trivial point in the circumstances). The whole development of Sunga sculpture is best regarded as a parallel rather than consecutive phenomenon to that of Gandhara.

For architecture, Pataliputra offers a stone capital in the form of a Greek anta capital and with Greek decoration – flame-palmettes, rosettes, tongues and bead-and-reel [**71**].[270] The same form appears elsewhere, better disguised.[271] It all seems logically to follow on from what was becoming apparent on the Mauryan columns. The early story that has Greek Saint ('Doubting') Thomas travel east and build a palace for the Indo-Parthian King Gondophernes, may conceal more prosaic contacts with Mediterranean practice that were encouraged by eastern kings. Monumentality was no novelty for Indians. The *Arthasastra* of Kautilya of the late 4th century BC already prescribed processional ways, colonnaded streets, arches, etc.[272]

Bodh Gaya was where the Buddha received enlightenment and was to be well provided with temples. The early one, from the Sunga period, has many classical features – the new styles of folded drapery, and a variety of subjects for roundels including a mermaid, centaur and winged elephant [72].[273]

Mathura was a Kushan capital and home to a vigorous sculptural school creating free-standing figures and reliefs. The bucolic scenes, of drunkenness and wild dancing, are as redolent of their Hellenistic ancestry as of much that we recognize readily in later Indian sculpture. The works are in their way more monumental than what we shall see in Gandhara, but there is certainly a connection.[274] A relief [73] perhaps indicates well enough the monumentality of

71 LEFT Anta capital of classical type from Pataliputra. 2nd cent. BC. (After *BAI*)

72 RIGHT A centaur on a relief roundel from Bodh Gaya. 2nd cent. BC. (After Coomaraswamy)

73 Relief from Mathura. 2nd cent. BC. (Delhi Museum)

the figure style and the character of the subject matter.[275] Wine is a constantly recurring theme in our story and this may be as good a place as any to reflect upon it. In early days the Greek god Dionysos' role was portrayed as that of a world-conqueror who spread the word about the importance of wine, and who found especial favour in India. Thus it was easy for a conqueror in the east like Alexander to become assimilated to him. It was said that, in celebratory games which Alexander held for an Indian philospher, Calanus, he included a contest in drinking unmixed wine, from the effects of which all the contestants eventually died, including the victor (a Greek, Promachos).[276] We have noted anecdotes relating to Greeks, wine and Alexander's progress – on Nisa, Meros, etc. There seems to have been at some level a real rapport in this respect at least between the Mediterranean world and the Indian.[277] Both Indian and Chinese sources praise the wines of the northwest, and, in Gandharan times, those of Kapisa (Begram). Of all the Indian gods Siva has most to do with

Dionysos in behaviour but direct assimilation probably takes the matter too far: enough to observe that Greek Dionysiac worship and practices found a ready echo in northwest India.[278] And there are other echoes of the Hellenistic world, as in the relief of an animal-eared man, naked, with serpent legs [74].[279] A tympanum bears a centaur-like monster with lion forepart and wings [75],[280]

74 Lintel relief: an animal-eared man with snake legs, from Mathura. 2nd cent. BC. (Mathura Museum. Drawing, author)

75 Tympanum from a doorway with two centauresses. From Mathura. 2nd cent. BC. (Boston, Museum of Fine Arts)

a good Hellenistic blend and here before a very Indian *makara* which will mate with the Greek *ketos*. The isolated appearance of the Roman *carnyx* trumpet at Sanchi may be a relic of Alexander's Gaulish mercenaries.[281]

Taxila and Gandhara

Chronologically we retrace here events already alluded to in discussion of the Greek record in Asia, but the site at Taxila is the perfect introduction to any account of later Greek fortunes in the east and their relationship to Buddhism and India, other than the earlier history of conflict, largely with Macedonians. The early associations of Taxila and similar sites with India to the south have also to be borne in mind.[282]

The history of the city of Taxila far predates what we recognize as Buddhist art but its finds and record are an essential introduction to it, and to what is recognized as Gandharan art. Its location between the upper reaches of the Indus and Jhelum rivers set it at a crossroads of several major routes, from northeastern India, from the west and Bactria, and from the steppe north.[283] The sprawling town included three city-sites, the Bhir Mound, which is the oldest, Sirkap where the Greeks built, and Sirsukh, of the Kushan period. It was already a major city when Alexander arrived and he is thought to have conversed with Brahmans there.[284] On Bhir Mound was, no doubt, the capital of Persia's richest satrapy, the Indian, and it was from the Aramaic script of the Persian Empire that Indian Kharoshti script was derived, as well as absorbing in time no little from the Greek alphabet.[285] Alexander spent time there, sacrificing and planning his progress farther east. Only after the move of the Bactrian Indo-Greeks southward are there excavated remains of Greek building – in what seems to be a deliberate bid to build a Greek city as substantial as Aï Khanoum (recently abandoned) had been, but at a time when Taxila was still a major Buddhist centre, having been established as such by Asoka himself in the mid-3rd century. Of the Greeks moving south it was Demetrios, then Eukratides, who promoted Taxila as a Greek capital for rather less than a century. King Menander was sufficiently acclimatized as to acquire some reputation as a Buddhist scholar, and called himself *soter* (saviour) on his coins. In his reign Greek rule probably reached its greatest extent. A successor, Antialkidas, is named by his ambassador Heliodoros on a column he dedicated at Besnagar in honour of Vishnu, inscribed 'Three are the steps to immortality which ... followed lead to heaven: self-control, self-denial and watchfulness'. The Greeks were clearly closely involved in the politics and ethos of Buddhism and north India. On coinage this is revealed in the use of Kharoshti beside Greek [50] and even the appearance of square coins, an Indian preference, but now for Greek kings.

The site at Sirkap suited Greek taste – a large, fairly flat area with an isolated 'acropolis', and defined by hills and streams. It was surrounded by a stone fortification wall some 3 miles (5 km) in length, and must have been an almost ideal version of those 'walled cities' in which the Greeks were said to live in Asia, even more so than Aï Khanoum. It had a broad Main Street running north–south for three-quarters of a mile (over a kilometre), to beside a major fortified gateway in the north, its Greek buildings replacing what amounted to a small suburb of the earlier non-Greek occupancy of the Bhir Mound. Later occupation has somewhat obscured details of the buildings of the Greek period but it is clear that they followed the expected pattern – symmetrical insulae of houses designed in the usual Greek manner with rooms set around an open courtyard. But the plans become less regular with time and the approach of the new Scythian/Parthian settlement, since the city was not abandoned once the Greeks had moved on. Not surprisingly, the Buddhist areas of Sirkap reveal much that is classical – a stupa whose body is simply a large Corinthian capital [76], and another where it is covered by an enormous acanthus leaf [77].[286]

Some 700 yards (650 m) north of the Sirkap city gate (at Jandial) lie the foundations of a temple of broadly Greek type, but it lacks the usual peripteral columns and instead has thick walls pierced by many windows. But there are the expected pairs of Ionic columns at the entrance [78] and, just within, at the door to the main oikos, it is divided into the expected pronaos and naos, behind which the mass of masonry suggests some towering superstructure, which is very difficult to envisage on an otherwise Greek building. The columns are well constructed, canonical Ionic but not fluted, the walls mainly coursed rubble, the upperworks no doubt wooden. The plan suggests a somewhat different

76 LEFT Model stupa at
Taxila with a Corinthian
capital supporting the dome.
2nd century BC (?). (After *Taxila*)

77 ABOVE Model stupa decorated
with classical acanthus leaves,
from Taxila. 2nd century BC (?).
(After *Taxila*)

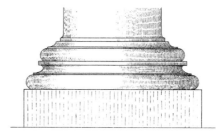

78 Ionic column capital and base
from the Jandial Temple, Taxila.
1st century AD (?). (After *Taxila*)

sort of compromise with local practice from that of the temple with niches at Aï Khanoum. Philostratos, writing about Apollonios of Tyana who visited India in the 1st century AD (see below), tells of a 100-ft (30-m) temple before the wall at Taxila, of shell-like stone (so, calcareous limestone or stuccoed?), with a small sanctuary and containing plaques illustrating the deeds of Alexander and the Indian King Poros. It is not wholly clear whether this is the Jandial temple. But the probability is that the building as we know it does not belong to the Greek period at Taxila but to a slightly later one, when Scythian/Saka or Parthian influence was strong, and that this may even be the source of its 'Greek' features.[287] As we have seen, in the 3rd century AD Saint Thomas supposedly built a palace there for an Indo-Parthian king, when also Apollonios visited the city and saw (he alleged) the altars to the Twelve Gods set up by Alexander on the River Beas.[288]

Among other sites of the region Charsada (Pushkalavati) should be mentioned as a mini-Taxila, yielding some rather less distinguished classicizing sculpture, but also a sealing from a gem with a classical Athena.[289]

The end of Greek rule at Taxila, or at least the end of the dominance of the Taxila site, comes with the spread of Parthian rule to the east, followed by the arrival of nomads from the north, part of the general southwards movement generated by the Yuehzhi, but in this case involving the Saka (Scythians). Yet their first king there in the mid-1st century BC, Maues, mints coins of Greek type on which he calls himself *basileus* in Greek and *maharaja* in Indian Kharoshti, and it is clear that the culture of Taxila long remained dominated by, first, its occupancy before the Greeks by Asokan Buddhism, and then by the Greeks themselves.[290] The Saka penetrated far into north India, before being replaced by the Parthians (Pahlavas). Maues was followed by the Saka dynasty of Azes, which ruled in the Indus Valley and Punjab down to AD 30. Of nomad peoples only the Yuehzhi seemed capable of developing a strong non-nomad society, even empire. Throughout this period Greekness was everywhere apparent, the language was spoken and written, the arts understood and practised, by Greeks and others.

The story, in the terms in which we are telling it, is demonstrated by the finds, and we can start from Taxila. Greek 'classical' style on objects of Greek type is the least common phenomenon, except on coinage, which has required separate treatment here in terms of both art and of Greek presence. What we find more often is Greek style and subjects translated in various degrees for objects or purposes not essentially Greek at all, not merely imitative of what might be regarded as imported goods but rather inspired by a contemporary and Greek view of what the customer required and understood. 'Gandhara' and its arts loom large enough here for the locality to give its name to many of the relevant arts and artifacts. One word of caution. The overall appearance of Gandharan stone sculptures is determined by the material, usually a relatively soft sandstone of a reddish-brown aspect – frankly dull. We must remember that many if not all were gilt, of which there are clear traces on numerous specimens, and there must have been much other colour as well. As with 'classical' art our eyes and so our judgment are easily misled by the monochrome appearance of works which originally were bright with colour and gold.

Stone palettes

A prime example of this lack of original decoration, and perhaps the earliest Gandharan manifestation of it, is provided by the little stone palettes, well represented at Taxila and on many other sites, and a common feature of museum collections worldwide. Trivial objects they may be, but they are worth some detailed attention here since they best demonstrate the range of Hellenistic figure devices copied in the east and the way they were adjusted, or not, for a different climate and religion. They are like small saucers with a decorative border and usually a plain underside. The shallow bowl is decorated with figures in relief, commonly over an open area below, which may feature a Greek palmette or eastern lotus, and in time the figures are set in smaller segments of the circle. We might assume that the cavities could serve as a repository for oil or unguents, a view reinforced by the minority which also admit separate small compartments. There is even a possible picture of their use, man to woman.[291] But their decoration does not reflect their use at all, and they are in this respect more like decorative miniature phialai with classical subjects in the tondos. They are made of relatively soft stone – steatite and schist – but the best are carefully turned to give a regular section. The general

84 Stone palette: Aphrodite chastises Eros; from Narai. 1st cent. BC. (London, British Museum 1973.6-18. W. 12 cm)

85 Stone palette: Herakles and Auge. 1st cent. BC. (London, Victoria & Albert Museum IS1218)

rampant lion and is accompanied by a dog.[303] He seems an easterner, with tunic and trousers, but the scene is familiar west to east in this period. Aphrodite chastising Eros [**84**] is a familiar although rare western motif.[304] More obvious is a Europa on a Zeus-bull, holding a thunderbolt.[305]

We have seen, and shall see again, that Herakles had a good career in the east. On the palette in ill. **85** it looks like him at the right, cowering beside his bow, and then the attendant woman might be Auge, not too unlike western

86 Stone palette: the death of Attis (?). From Taxila. 1st cent. BC.
(Kansas City. Nelson Gallery. W. 12 cm)

renderings.[306] He figures also as a drunkard supported by two women and attended by a lion.[307] And similarly, busts only, on a fragmentary rectangular palette.[308] The scene in ill. **86** would pose questions of identification wherever found. A near-naked youth lies prostrate, perhaps dead, over the body of a boar and being attended by satyrs – perhaps he is Meleager but his undress suggests Attis, the emasculated consort of Kybele, famously killed by a boar.[309] A snake-legged giant wielding boulders [**87**] is directly in the tradition of the Great Altar at Pergamum, but has a female version too.[310] A Poseidon with trident appears attended by women,[311] and there is even Eros riding a swan.[312]

Some subjects seem certainly of Greek inspiration but defy closer identity. The figure in ill. **88** should be Herakles since his quiver, club (below) and lionskin (head seen from above at the right) would make this so.[313] But

87 Stone palette: a giant.
1st cent. BC (Private, Colmar.
After Francfort. W. 10 cm)

88 Stone palette: Herakles
and Omphale? 1st cent. BC.
(Bull Collection. After
Francfort)

he is unexpectedly, and very oddly, dressed, perhaps even wearing a pointed cap like that worn by the countryside aggressor already noted.[314] The victim looks queenly and might be Omphale, but she was attacked in her palace not a woodland. One wonders whether the creator had an easy explanation – he is master of a style, part Greek (the man's head), part eastern, of a type not easily paralleled.

Greek subjects especially adjusted to local interests form a larger class. Of these the most notable is the *ketos* sea monster, which was invented in Greece in the 5th century BC. There it had a long fishy body, two flippers or forelegs (more or less feline), a head with a long muzzle, tall ears, a louring forehead, and was in due course given the option of horns and a beard. The body can boast seaweed or acanthus-like frills. We have met one already on a probably Bactrian *phalera* [53] and it proves to have a distinguished history elsewhere as well as on our current concern, the palettes. It, and its Nereid companion, are common subjects for the tondi of Hellenistic plate (for example, a group found in South Russia, neighbouring Central Asia).[315] In Greece the *ketos* often serves as the mount for a Nereid who may carry new armour for Achilles or a cup. She may appear dressed, rather formal, or near-naked, often sprawled on the beast as commonly in later Hellenistic art. Both types appear in the east, as well as other riders. Most like the Nereid is a woman in Greek dress, usually holding a cup like a phiale [89].[316] She once seems to feed the monster from the phiale, which is something a Nereid might do.[317] On others there are two groups. But the other more exotic naked nymphs also appear, generally showing their backs and dressed only with the crossed ribbons derived from Hellenistic Greek jewelry and much favoured in Gandharan/Indian art. There are fine statuettes of such (un)dressed figures from Taxila, as well as many reliefs which we shall come to shortly, and one palette has the bare lady, back to us, seated beside two musicians, one of whom leans on a Greek lyre.[318] But first the *ketea*. On other palettes the girl is clambering on to the beast from the side, as in PL. XL[319] – a very imaginative pose, and on a piece where the gilding has been comparatively well preserved; on another she is comfortably settled [90].[320] But both are attended by an Eros, showing that the measure of Greek identity has not been forgotten.[321] The nude back view could easily have been

89 Stone palette: a Nereid on a *ketos*. (Alsdorf Collection. After Czuma 1985)

90 Stone palette: a Nereid mounting a *ketos*, greeted by Cupid. From Taxila. 1st cent. BC. (Taxila Museum 175/1932-3. After Francfort. W. 8 cm)

91 Stone palette: a two-tailed Triton holding a dolphin embraces a naked Nereid.
1st cent. BC. (New York, Metropolitan Museum 1987.142.4. W. 11.43 cm)

suggested by the common Greek motif of a naked Nereid, seen from the back,
clambering on to or clutching the side of a hippocamp. One variant palette has
her alone on a hippocamp, not a *ketos*,[322] and on others the *ketos* has acquired
a bull's head,[323] or a winged lion forepart,[324] or a panther's head with the girl
holding a snake (or dress?).[325] On one she is accompanied by a real Triton [**91**].[326]
What is most remarkable here is that the Triton, who seems almost to carry
her, is holding a dolphin on his arm, a motif we have already met in ill. **63**
and one with possible associations with the River Oxus. Once the Nereid is
winged,[327] and on one fragment she formed part of a group.[328] The popularity
of the motif on the palettes is difficult to fathom, unless, for the more formal
one, a local identity had been devised (like the Triton/Oxus); the nakedness of
the others is in keeping with much from north India of this date, such as the

ivories from Begram [103] and a number of somewhat bucolic reliefs [111]. We shall see that the *ketos* itself will find its kin in the Indian *makara*.

There are later 'Parthian' palettes, still very Greek in spirit and many retaining Greek subjects, where the Nereid may be replaced by Eros or a youth, and once there are two youths on *ketea* holding cups [PL. XXXVIII],[329] or where the monster's head has become leonine and lost its special ketoid character.[330] A more typical subject for the 'Parthian' is a drinking couple, such as is found on other Parthian works (buckles, etc.),[331] with the remote possibility of being an echo of paired Dionysos and Ariadne, as on PL. XXXI of much the same date.

The whole class starts with an iconography of pure Greek inspiration, deriving immediately from Indo-Greek Bactria and sometimes quite novel. It comes to accept more and more the subjects and even the style of later rulers in Gandhara – Parthians, Indians. It gives a vivid demonstration of the ease with which Greek subjects could be copied, adapted and acclimatized in non-Greek environments, and apparently become accepted as 'native'.

It is tempting to associate with the palette form some roundels in silver with Greek ovolo borders, figuring a goddess with a child on her lap on a bird-topped throne but in a more 'Indian' style of the early years AD [PL. XXXIX] – she is the local version of a mother-goddess type whose general appearance and history ranges from the Mediterranean to the China Seas.[332]

Gems and seals

Tantalizingly, much of what we might reasonably regard as Greek production in the Gandhara area has no excavated context. This is commonly the case with seal stones, yet they are an important source of evidence for the diffusion of types. We have already considered the 'Greco-Persian gems' of the period of Persian domination [11–13]. The type did not die with the Persian Empire, and although new 'Hellenistic' styles soon found their way east, there was a very strong survival of the Greco-Persian, in what I have called the Bern Group.[333] These retain the scaraboid shape, rarely the tabloid, and their style tends to exaggerate the bulbous carving (*a globolo*) of some of the earlier series. Subjects include fewer with human figures although there are glimpses still of the Macedonian. One has a pure Greco-Persian cavalry duel [92].[334] The Persian

92, 93 Impressions of seals: a jasper scaraboid from Ephesus showing a Persian horseman attacking a Greek, and a chalcedony scaraboid showing a zebu bull. 2nd/1st cent. BC. (Oxford, Ashmolean Museum 1892.1596. W. 27 mm; St Petersburg, Hermitage Museum. W. 15 mm.)

seated ladies persist, but there are also a few seals with scenes of sexual activity that seem almost a Greek comment on superficial Persian respectability. Most subjects are animal and they soon begin to include types such as the eastern zebu bull [93].[335] There are also finger rings in the style, commonly with the seated-lady motif. They are well diffused in the east, even to Ceylon (Sri Lanka), but it is hard to tell just how late they might run. Some are certainly contemporary with the Taxilan [95] (see below), and their immediate successors, so they seem to represent a quite vigorous production which chose to cling still to old Greco-Persian manners rather than the new Hellenistic. And they are not confined to the east of the old empire. Far to the west there is a cylinder showing Celtic mercenary troops and inscribed in Aramaic.[336]

The more elaborate and heavy Hellenistic finger rings were also being produced with subjects of mixed origin and style. One gold ring, still of the old oval shape, carries a dressed woman with a wreath and a version of a satyr holding grapes, a slightly distorted rendition of a purely Greek subject. Some are all-metal like one with seated and standing figures that seem broadly Greek in style but Indian in subject [94].[337] Others have elaborately decorated hoops with relief figures, such as one where the sides of the hoop bear low-relief groups of the big Garuda bird carrying a figure,[338] a scene which might derive from the Greek group of Zeus' eagle carrying Ganymede. In this case the bezel

94 Silver finger ring: a woman offers a jug to another, seated. Inscribed in Kharoshti (Eilenberg Coll., Metropolitan Museum. H. 29 mm.)

features a stone intaglio with a countrified version of a Greek Aphrodite and a half-finished figure (?), such as was a frequent subject for these eastern stones well into centuries AD and to as far away as Ceylon.

But there is more of better Greek, but eastern pedigree. The most notable example is a brilliant portrait of Alexander proclaimed as of eastern manufacture both by its very rare material (elbaite, a variety of tourmaline) and the presence of a tiny inscription in the Indian Kharoshti script at the neckline [**PL. VIII**]. A sardonyx bought in Peshawar has a Hellenistic Aphrodite and is inscribed 'of Diodoros'.[339] A seal-engraver at Taxila left three specimens of his work which relate to the Greco-Roman in style and subject but not material [**95**].[340] At Tillya Tepe (1st century AD) there are classical subjects worked in turquoise, the local material (notably from Chorasmia), as well as

95 Three seals from Taxila featuring stags, two attacked by lions. 2nd/1st cent. BC. (After *GGFR*)

96 Turquoise cameo head of Herakles. 2nd cent. BC. (Missouri University)

97 Intaglio impression from northwest Pakistan showing Tyche, with cornucopia. 2nd cent. BC. (Victoria & Albert Museum 14.1948.408A. Photo, author)

gold finger rings, with Athenas and inscribed in a rather provincial Greek script [PL. XLIII].[341] A turquoise cameo of Herakles' head (probably copied from a coin) combines the new local material with the new hero for the east [96].[342] The head of his lover Omphale wearing his lionskin cap appears on a cameo from Akra, Pakistan [PL. XLIV].[343] From the same regions is a fine intaglio with a plump indianized Tyche [97].[344] Later comes a fine frontal Buddha head in a ruby-like corundum.[345]

Given the Greek penchant for seal-engraving with figures and small groups, rather than the more hieratic styles of Mesopotamia, we should not be surprised that the genre was well received in Gandhara and north India. The Greco-Persian style dies hard, often embellished with the Indian/oriental swastika or taurine (bull-head) sign. There is a plethora of classical subjects in shapes of classical type in our area, serving, it seems, both Indo-Greeks and Indians, who modestly adjust the style for sometimes more flamboyant figures.[346] Many intaglios, notably in glass, present local renderings of the most popular classical subjects – such as Herakles and the Lion, Pegasus,[347] or Nike. A seal impression in Oxford bears a long Kushan inscription, dating it to the 2nd/3rd century AD, and bears an unmistakable Herakles fighting one of the horses of Diomedes,

98 Seal impression. Herakles with one of the horses of Diomedes. 1st cent. AD. (Oxford, Ashmolean Museum AN 1953.131)

99 Chalcedony seal impression showing Tyche/Hariti with a child. 1st cent. AD (After Callieri. Drawing, author)

in the familiar Greek group and in a broadly classical style [98].[348] Among the intaglios we are as likely to find a Greek Pegasus as an Indian zebu bull, and, as in sculpture, a Hariti masquerading as a Greco-Roman Tyche/Fortuna.[349] The classical subjects are only slightly adjusted, even those also bearing a Kharoshti inscription; we have, for example, a chalcedony with an enthroned Tyche/ Hariti with cornucopia attended by an Eros-like child [99].[350] There are no few collections of such seals and sealings betraying a mixture of Greek, Greco-Persian and simply Indian styles and choices of subject.[351]

Jewelry

Jewelry was no less affected by Greek types, it seems. Bactrian-Greek arts included the jeweller's, and many basic types recur or are copied. There are gold spiral bracelets of Greek type, tipped with the head of a snake, sea monster (*ketos*) or crocodile, and others with the Greek artist's signature and a Greek weight record.[352]

There is considerable similarity west and east, sometimes in details such as earrings – Erotes as earrings had a long currency east of the Mediterranean, as in Parthian Nimrud[353] – and there is more than a superficial similarity between the undress of Greek figures and the Gandhara ladies seated at a drinking party [111] as well as the nymphs we have seen clambering on to sea monsters on palettes. The near-nude look for women came naturally in a climate such as that of north India and with the importance of fertility goddesses, just as it did in Greece where wealthy women were would-be Aphrodites, and, at least for the courtesan market, dress of hardly more than chains of gold linking ornate buckles, pectorals and the like, clearly occupied the time and invention of goldsmiths. This elegant style of undress seems well represented especially in western Asia Minor but is common to the whole Hellenistic world and very closely copied in the undress afforded women at Sanchi, on Begram ivories and on palettes.

One purely Indian jewelry type is the necklet with matching terminals centre front, with some central jewel or other decoration. PL. XXXVI (also ill. 1) seems to be one such, a little winged figure, rather like a sphinx, wearing body jewelry of Greek/Indian type. But this is a reading sphinx, such as Oedipus encountered, and on the scroll she holds we read, in Greek letters – ΘEA – 'goddess' – an Indian *devi*. She is related to gold earrings found in the east, local versions of the Hellenistic.[354] In a similar position on a Gandhara Bodhisattva appear the familiar *ketos* heads, while a classical bust, perhaps Herakles, sits at the centre of the same figure's collar.[355] Commoner are small figures or groups of classical subjects in gold, barely if at all adjusted for the east: at Taxila,

100 Gold statuette of Aphrodite and Eros, from Gandhara. 1st cent. BC/AD. (London, British Museum 1962.11-12.1. H. 3.8 mm)

a boy and girl group that recall Eros and Psyche, and later at Tillya Tepe the Aphrodite sporting wings and an Asian caste mark on her forehead [**PL. XXXV**], and another with butterfly wings (as worn by Psyche in the west) and holding an Eros [**PL. XXXIV**].[356] A more completely in-the-round gold Aphrodite has Eros clambering up her leg [**100**].[357] A naked, dancing, kissing couple accompanied by Eros are wholly Hellenistic, in relief on a blue glass roundel.[358]

Plate

A notable feature of finds of silver plate in the east has been the number of late Hellenistic drinking vessels with elaborate figure decoration and a rich repertoire of classical subjects – and we may bear in mind also the casts of such material found at Begram in later years (see below). The common shape, kantharoid, has its effect too. One in a hoard has a fine Dionysiac and theatrical worship scene [**101**],[359] and from the same hoard are cups with centaurs, an old Heraklean/Dionysiac lyre-player seated on a lion, the rending of Pentheus by three maenads, a party of Erotes and rustic scenes. Cups with horizontal fluting recall the Persian.[360] Greek, Persian, Scythian and Indian names appear on them, and weights are given in various standards, Greek to Indian.[361] These give an important clue to one of the sources of unusual and up-to-date Hellenistic motifs to inspire Greek and local artists.

101 The decoration on a silver cup showing a scene of the worship of Dionysos. 1st cent. BC. (Kreitman Collection. After *Crossroads*. Drawing, Marion Cox)

102 Silver cup from Buddhigharra featuring a drinking scene. 2nd cent. AD.
(London, British Museum OA 1937.3-19.1. Diam. 25.1 cm)

A phiale (western shape) from Buddhigharra (Punjab) [102] offers what
amounts to an Indian Dionysos and Ariadne drinking in a vineyard,[362] and with
the wavy fluting we see on western plate. The style of the figures is in marked
contrast with that in ill. **101**, which is pure Greek.

The ordinary pottery of the Kushan world owes much to the tradition
of Greco-Bactrian.[363] To the north, it is remarkable how, even earlier, Greek
potters in the east seem to have kept in step with developments in the west,
even in the common wares.[364]

Begram

Before looking more closely at the 'Gandhara style', there is a site which is as
important as Taxila and which illustrates the distant connections of the area
over much the same period, the 1st to 3rd centuries AD. It is Begram, a palace
site in which two rooms were found walled up and full of objects that seem

to present a good cross section of the trading interests of Gandhara in this period.[365] A few are purely western of the early Roman period.[366] More revealing are eastern works that betray strongly the effect of Greek arts. The many ivory reliefs from furniture are broadly in the style of the Sunga stupas and their successors in north India. A splendid ivory plaque with incised figures of Indian women, largely naked, is bordered by a pattern of rinceaux with birds which is purely Hellenistic, while at the corners are compositions of combined animal heads just like the so-called *grylli* of contemporary western gem-engraving [103],[367] and some of the whole figures of women copy western subjects more closely – one wringing her wet hair like any Aphrodite.[368] Free-standing ivory figures of

103 Ivory plaque from Begram depicting women at leisure, with a floral border. 2nd cent. AD. (Kabul Museum)

women manage to combine western drapery conventions with a marked degree of the Indian voluptuous treatment of the female form, and broadly resemble a figure found in Pompeii, which is far stiffer in its pose.[369]

An unusual group of objects in the rooms is of plaster casts made from metal vases and figurines, displaying a very good range of relief figure styles of late Hellenistic type and of western origin.[370] It is not easy to understand their purpose but the practice of making casts from important relief plate seems widespread and was remarked by Pliny (*Nat. Hist.* 33. 157, apropos of pieces too valuable to cast in metal). They might have served as models for local metalsmiths but what we can distinguish of such work obviously made in the east is never quite so ambitious. Moreover, it would not explain why, among the relief casts, there is a cast of a life-size human foot. It is more as though a set of casts in use by some western artist had been carried east as curious works of art, or simply for their potential as decoration. A very few similar casts have been found elsewhere in the east. We should probably not overvalue them as evidence for sources of classicism in the east.

Otherwise Begram offers a fine range of good early Roman (or Alexandrian) glass, much of it painted and one piece showing in relief the Pharos (Lighthouse of Alexandria) [104],[371] which may be a clue to the source of much of the rest; and there are small western bust bronzes for perfume, even a Roman type of folding chair (*curule*) on which a later Kushan king may be shown seated.[372]

Greek and/or Roman – a memo

Inevitably, for our western comparanda, we turn to the Roman world, which by now encompassed all of Greece and much of the Near East. For Mesopotamia and parts of Persia the most impressive monuments are the great cities modelled on a Roman imperial style with triumphal arches, massive forums and temples and colonnaded streets. But we might remember that this is an area which had been used to monumental architecture from long before Rome was founded, and, even given that 'classical' architecture began with Greece, that this is no good reason to associate Greeks especially with the new building. Moreover, closer inspection reveals how much of the

104 Painted glass model of the Lighthouse (Pharos) at Alexandria, from Begram.
(Kabul Museum. H. 16.8 cm)

east is still expressed in both the detail and use of the buildings. A temple of Jupiter is also one of Baal, and often it is local religious practice rather than anything specifically Roman (let alone Greek) that determined the layout, use and fortunes of such buildings.[373]

Beyond Persia it is a different matter. Real Greek presence is obvious, and for the most part what we observe copies most closely the work of those parts of the eastern Roman Empire which were still Greek in language and tradition – more of Alexandria and Aphrodisias than of Italy, and stylistically there is a certain divide still between east and west in the arts of the Mediterranean. Contrast the effects of Roman metropolitan (in Italy) art in Roman Britain or Gaul. In Asia Minor particularly the Romans were very active in the early centuries AD and on non-military matters. Great new temples and civic structures were built, especially under Hadrian, who himself visited Asia Minor twice. This activity certainly may have involved some degree of Roman presence, tempered by a Greek population with skills in architecture. But it was the Hellenistic tradition which survived and was influential to the east,[374] where Hadrian's successors were more preoccupied with Parthia. Intellectually the Greeks of Asia Minor were if anything more ambitious than the scholars of their homeland – philosophers (Dio Chrysostom, Epictetus), historians (Strabo, Pausanias, Arrian), doctors (Galen), all born in Asia Minor.[375] On the ground, Latin inscriptions are very rare indeed.

When it comes to details in the representational arts, early Roman art certainly developed the notion of continuous narrative, the same figure appearing in successive scenes, a style which the physical disposition of Greek art seldom encouraged except on some series of temple metopes. It well suited series of narrative scenes of the life of the Buddha, but these are generally more naively composed. There is certainly some reason to look for direct inspiration from the arts of imperial Rome even beyond what was developed in the Greek world, although there is little if any evidence of such 'Roman' transmission so far to the east. In fact Indian types of narrative art can be even more sophisticated than the Roman.[376] In matters of dress the distinctive style of wearing the Roman toga is not adopted rather than variations of the usual Hellenistic Greek himation.[377]

In general there is a great deal 'classical' of the early centuries AD in the east which, in Mediterranean terms, one could judge as much graecized Roman as Greek – notably the many bronze statuettes of gods.[378] However, the overwhelmingly Greek character of all the coinage of this period, and well into the centuries AD, and the absence of Roman coins or Latin, speaks decisively for the principal source of classicism in the area beyond Persia.[379]

Yet Augustan art in particular is picked out by some scholars as the inspiration for Gandharan arts. In its way it exemplifies what Greek artists brought to Rome, to be developed for quite different purposes. Almost all the artists' names on monumental art of the period in Italy are Greek and what they brought west was practised still at home in developing Hellenistic/Roman styles. It would not be easy to say of any Gandharan motif that there was more of Rome than Greece in it, nor does it much matter, and Roman motifs, such as the wolf with Romulus and Remus, were current throughout the Roman Empire. The immediate access to the east was via Egypt and Greek lands, where the Roman too could promote Greek arts at a high level (for example, the emperor Hadrian) rather than overland through Mesopotamia and Persia. But even allowing for the strong Greek tradition in architecture there are certainly some signs of knowledge of Roman architectural practice.[380]

For India a new route was opened through the Red Sea and across to the Indian Ocean (which the Greeks called the Red Sea), by open sea rather than along the Persian Gulf, aiming for Barygaza (Bharuch). Its starting point was among the 'Greek Egyptians' of Alexandria, and it moved a Greek to write a sailor's guide to the Ocean – in Greek.[381] This will have stimulated further trade from India, notably in precious stones, which suddenly become more varied in their range in the Mediterranean world. Some Roman pottery and coins arrive in the east too, but most conspicuously in the south (including Ceylon) rather than the north, where connections seem mainly with the east Roman/Greek world. Pliny says that India received at least five million silver sesterces annually, selling back at a hundredfold profit.[382] Alexandria (which the writer Lawrence Durrell called 'the capital of Asiatic Europe'), remained a key factor in all this commerce, and a 2nd-century AD papyrus deals with loans made there to finance trade with the Ganges Valley – spices, ivory, textiles.[383] And the

Greco-Egyptian link is nicely illustrated by a classical bronze 1st-century BC/AD figure of Harpocrates, found at Taxila [105].[384]

The story of the Greek Eudoxos is illuminating (Strabo 2.3.4), whether or not, as alleged, he ever circumnavigated Africa. He worked in Egypt for the Ptolemaic court (which also robbed him of precious stones and spices) on the India run, and his cargoes out included craftsmen, dancing girls and doctors. The Indians called their Greek (and probably any western) visitors Yavanas (Yona, Yonaka) using a version of the old term (Yauna) employed first for them by the Assyrians in Syria a millennium before.[385] The evidence for trade links in the early centuries AD is strong, with envoys passing west and east to 1st- and 2nd-century Roman emperors.[386] But Greek, not Latin, scripts are in use, notably by the Kushans, and one of the earliest Kushan coins showing the Buddha as a figure (and in the Greek manner) rather than a symbol, names him in Greek letters, BODDO [106].[387] Strangely, the Greek alphabet continued in

105 Bronze figure of Harpocrates from Taxila. 1st cent. AD. (Taxila Museum. After Harle)

166

106 Gold Kushan coin showing the Buddha. (London, British Museum. W. 20 mm)

occasional use for non-Greek languages; it (and Aramaic, which had largely disappeared) may have seemed in its way more easy to use and understand than some local scripts, and it seems to have been spoken even as an official language in the Kushan Empire.[388] An inscription in Greek letters records a predecessor of Kanishka setting up temples and the installation of figures of gods and kings.[389] Aelian (12.48) said that the Indians transcribe the poems of Homer into their own language and recite them. Whether this practice could be a source for artistic invention also is another matter; I am sceptical.[390]

Overall, Warwick Ball's account of the problem[391] is exemplary and he allows me to quote his last paragraph: 'Most of all it must be pointed out that the controversies over Greco-Bactrian versus direct Roman versus Irano-Hellenistic origins for Gandharan art are not in conflict: *all* hypotheses must be substantially correct. None of the hypotheses so far argued can by themselves account for the unquestionable western character of the style. But the combination of *all* forces and influences is the only possible explanation for perhaps the most extraordinary syncretism in art history. To argue for one hypothesis over the others is to miss the point.'

The 'Gandhara style' in sculpture

The Gandhara style is generally applied to the relief sculpture from the stupas of Gandhara,[392] and to a range of statuettes and reliefs with comparable figures. Exploration of it has become a fashionable pursuit for both classicists and scholars of Asia. It is taken to exemplify the effect of Greek sculptural forms on Buddhist art of the 1st to 3rd centuries AD, in the period of Kushan rule, and this, indeed, it does very well. It may be regarded as a Kushan-Indian invention based on the pervasive classical ambience, and distinct from Kushan dynastic arts, which are more closely dependent on northern and even Parthian practices.[393] Immediate predecessors must be sought in works discussed already, even the earlier palettes, and even far to the north at a site like Khalchayan, north of the Oxus, which has produced classicizing works displaying a surprising range of naturalism and expression, mainly in clay, even a helmeted goddess.[394] These are perhaps more Parthian than earliest Gandhara/Kushan, but we do not know what by way of major sculpture might have graced the home of the prince of the Tillya Tepe graves in the 1st century AD.

The phenomenon is worth a moment's thought. Classical art, its realistic poses, compositions and sometimes adjusted identities, are being used to demonstrate a different religion and mythological world in a vastly different environment. Something of the same sort was to happen again, but without the environmental change, when classical art was discovered by Renaissance artists and used to illustrate the Bible and Christian traditions. A major difference is that the emotional power of classicism, rather than its compositions and narrative, was not as deeply exploited in the east as it was to be in Christian Europe, although much of the power of calm figure groups is captured in some of the earlier reliefs, as also the techniques of narrative.

The main series of the Gandharan reliefs are generally small and come from stairways on stupas, whence there are also some triangular corner-pieces, or from pillars, but there are more monumental works too. The stone is dull and often dark, uninspiring (mainly phyllite). We have to remember again that, as for most parts of the ancient world, what we see is not what antiquity saw. All classical and Indian sculpture was highly coloured, the classical realistically, the Indian probably more lividly and much like the highly painted Hindu temples of the modern world. Gilding too was widely employed. The Gandhara stone sculpture rarely shows signs of the gilding, even less of the colour, but we should judge it in terms which allow for an appearance very different indeed from what we see today. The copying by Renaissance artists of classical works from which time had removed all colour has generated an expectation in the west, and wherever western art has penetrated, that sculpture, in the round

107 Relief of a man assaulting a woman, from Butkara. 2nd cent. AD. (After *ACSS*)

or relief, should be blank – whence the appearance of all classicizing architectural sculpture, monuments and memorials, which accounts for most of what
is seen publicly in the west today. This gives us such a false view of antiquity,
which was a bright and colourful place, in Athens as much as India.

One of the earliest sources is Butkara in the Swat Valley.[395] The erotic relief
in ill. **107** is very Greek in spirit and detail of dress (notice the female figleaf).[396]
Some of the earliest reliefs from the Buddhist monuments present subjects in
which it is indeed difficult to detect Buddhism at all, rather than a Greek cer-
emonial of some sort involving prince and consort. Such is seen in ill. **108**, where

the dress is wholly Greek and a man and woman are attended by others, one bearing a large cup.[397] There are several similar reliefs centring on a senior male and with, it seems, a woman being presented. Where dress is concerned the treatment of drapery can sometimes look even like 'sub-archaic' Greek, with the zigzag folds which had also attracted Achaemenid artists. A striking example is a piece from Mathura.[398] The feature may indeed be derived from Persian graeciz-ing practice but it is more probably a reflection of the renewed interest in such archaic patterning in the Greek world itself – the 'neo-Attic' archaizing styles of the 1st century BC, which exaggerated such patterning. Another feature of such reliefs and much else Gandharan is their commitment to frontality where, in the classical world, most figures would be presented in profile. This may be due in part to earlier Indian traditions and in part to the preference for frontality by now found throughout the Parthian world.

What we might judge to be Dionysiac themes were especially popular, affect-ing style and content.[399] A festive group, with music, includes a male with a cup and very bare body and a woman carrying a Greek wine amphora, none too accurately copied [109].[400] A Dionysiac group closely based on western models

108 Relief of couples in Greek style from Takht-I Bahi. 1st/2nd cent. AD. (London, British Museum OA 1900.4-14.13. W. 33 cm)

109 Relief with drinkers and musicians, from Hadda. 1st/2nd cent. AD.
(Paris, Guimet Museum)

110 Relief with a drunken Indian Silenos on a mule. 2nd cent. AD.
(Private coll. After Boardman, *Nostalgia*)

has a typical drunken Silenus on his donkey, offered wine by a dressed Indian maenad [110], a commonplace of the Mediterranean world in the Hellenistic and later corpus of such scenes, notably in the Triumph of Dionysos, celebrating the god's victories in the east.[401] The 'Stacy Silenus' and Palikhera block feature corpulent drinking Sileni accompanied by figures in Indian dress

111 Relief in the shape of a stool side and showing drinking couples. 2nd cent. AD. (Lahore Museum 1914)

holding grapes and offering appropriate support, the former from the Mathura area demonstrating a link already noted.[402] These were pedestal blocks designed to support large bowls, and they show how the themes could be adapted to an only slightly different environment. The bare-backed ladies and their bibulous companions have been remarked already apropos of their appearance on the Gandhara palettes.[403] A relief in Lahore offers the near-naked ladies at feast again [111] on a relief of interesting shape, the sides taking the form of lion legs. This is simply a copy of the side of a classical footstool, and the Indian versions do not always bother to show the leonine details as here.[404]

Groups of marine heroes appear, posing like Greek athletes but with exaggerated physique and acanthoid frills at the waist which seem a Greek addition to the human and monstrous in the east.[405] Other reliefs are simply new renderings of the putti and garlands which decorated Roman-period sarcophagi of the Greek world,[406] or versions of the architectural rinceaux of the west[407] such as we have seen already decorating an Indian ivory at Begram [103]. The putti with garlands persist even on to the Kanishka casket-reliquary [112].[408]

112 Replica of the Kanishka casket (1st cent. AD), copper; original from Shah-jik-i-Dheri, Peshawar. (London, British Museum OA 1880-270. H. 18 cm)

113 Relief of children (Cupids) with swags. 1st/2nd cent. AD. (London, British Museum OA 1940.7.-13.1)

The way the garlands often have swags of flowers or fruit hanging from them [113][409] is a feature of sarcophagi from Asia Minor from the mid-2nd century AD on, rather than Italy. The hellenized figure groups seem almost a logical succession to the ivory rhyta of Nisa [42–45]. And when, exceptionally, we find a rendering of the Trojan horse being pushed towards the gates of Troy [114], we

114 Relief showing the Trojan Horse before the gates of Troy, barred by Cassandra. From Mardan. 1st/2nd cent. AD. (London, British Museum OA 1990.10-13.1. W. 25.4 cm)

have an iconographic scheme of purely western inspiration, even if not very closely matched there, enhanced by a thoroughly oriental Cassandra trying to bar the way into the city.[410] And equally distanced from the original is another representation of the same scene where there is just a Cassandra holding a cup (?) and the horse with a warrior emerging from its neck, owing nothing to the west beyond the story.[411]

Corner-pieces for the stupa steps are decorated sometimes with classical figures of Tritons and the like, whose tailed bodies fit the angular frame well [**115**].[412] Somewhat larger reliefs in the same style concentrate on the Buddha and his adventures, and also his entourage, often including an attendant Herakles as Parthian Vajrapani, with thunderbolt (ex-club), as attendant.[413] A far odder Herakles/Vajrapani figure appears on a relief in an architectural setting, cloaked, booted and hooded.[414] Vajrapani's iconographic derivation from Herakles is as striking as his frequent attendance on the Buddha in art.[415] There is also a far more classical young Herakles with diminished lionskin from Swat [**116**].[416]

A recurrent subject is noted also elsewhere here (p. 154): a great eagle lifting a human figure. In the Greek world this is the Zeus-eagle carrying off Ganymede. In the east the figure is female, and may be an Anahita.[417] This

115 Stair-corner relief with a winged Triton, from Peshawar. 1st/2nd cent. AD. (London, British Museum OA 1889.10-16.2. H. 28.5 cm)

practice of borrowing a classical scheme or group for a different cast is carried further in relief groups which show a pillar being lifted (to measure or crush the Buddha, it is not clear which) and are based on classical groups of satyrs lifting a Dionysos herm, or Cupids with Herakles' club, or raising a trophy.[418]

Many of the small reliefs are flanked by boxed columns which are versions of the classical Corinthian. They may be inspired by the corner columns of some classical sarcophagi. In the east their capitals are less basket-like (an exception being the stupa-capital in ill. **76**), and have their

116 Relief showing a young Herakles, his head with a halo. From Swat. 2nd cent. AD. (After *Fest. Fischer*)

leaves flatter and spread, the whole subdivided horizontally rather than vertically. Larger versions appear in the round and these may entertain figures seated among the leaves, even the Buddha [117],[419] or a splendid version of the reclining Herakles/Verethagna with his cup, as he had appeared long before at Bisitun [38], on a capital from Karatepe on the Oxus [118].[420] There are several at Butkara.[421] From the market and somewhat later in date is a set of three with the Buddha and attendants.[422] And then there is the love affair between

117 Corinthian capital with the figure of the Buddha. From Jamalgarhi. 2nd cent. AD. (London, British Museum OA 1880.357)

118 Corinthian capital with the figure of reclining Herakles. From Karatepe. 2nd cent. AD. (After *ACSS*)

XXXI Gold and turquoise plaque from Tillya Tepe. Dionysos and Ariadne, crowned by a Victory, ride a lion. A satyr gleans drops from the god's cup. 1st century AD. (Kabul Museum. 7 × 6.5 cm)

OVERLEAF

XXXII ABOVE Gold plaques. A fully armed warrior stands in an arbour, with lions, from Tillya Tepe. 1st century AD. (Kabul Museum. 9 × 6.3 cm)

XXXIII BELOW LEFT Gold hairpin tops, of acanthus and lotus leaves, from Tillya Tepe. 1st century AD. (Kabul Museum. Diam. 7.5 cm)

XXXIV BELOW RIGHT Gold plaque. Winged Aphrodite with Eros, standing between pillars. From Tillya Tepe. 1st century AD. (Kabul Museum. 4.5 × 2.5 cm)

FOLLOWING PAGE

XXXV LEFT Gold plaque. Winged Aphrodite leaning on a column. From Tillya Tepe. 1st century AD. (Kabul Museum. H. 5.0 cm)

XXXVI RIGHT Gold finial from a necklet. A siren holds a scroll inscribed ΘEA ('goddess'). See also ill. 1. (Kreitman Coll. After *Crossroads*. H. 3.8 cm)

XXXVIII ABOVE Stone palette showing two youths riding *ketea*. 2nd century AD. (Oxford, Ashmolean Museum EA 1996.82. Photo, Museum)

XXXIX BELOW Silver roundel showing an enthroned goddess with a child on her lap, in an ovolo border. (Oxford, Ashmolean Museum EA 1977.22. Photo, Museum)

XL Stone palette showing a woman climbing onto the flank of a *ketos* and greeted by Cupid. Traces of gilding. (Unknown whereabouts)

XXXVII Stone pillar capital from Sarnath. Lions on a plinth decorated with rosettes, a horse and zebu, over a bell-shaped member. 3rd century BC. (Calcutta, India Museum H. 2.15 m)

XLI Stone head of a Bodhisattva from an acrolithic statue. 2nd century AD. (Ortiz Collection. H. 58 cm)

XLII Clay head of a Bodhisattva, from Tapa Shutor. 2nd century AD. (New York, Metropolitan Muuseum 1986.2. Photo, author)

XLIII Two gold ring bezels (one with silver centre) showing the goddess Athena and inscribed with her name, from Tillya Tepe. 1st century AD. (Kabul Museum. 1.6 × 1.2, 3 × 2.2 cm)

XLIV Onyx cameo showing the head of Omphale wearing Herakles' lion skin cap, from Akra. (London, British Museum 1893.0502.1)

XLV ABOVE Sasanian gilt silver cup showing Herakles tipping the boar onto Eurystheus who hides in a pot. 5th/6th cent. AD. (Ortiz Collection. Diam. 19.9 cm)

XLVI LEFT Sardonyx cameo showing a Sasanian king defeating a Roman. 5th cent. BC. (Paris, Bibl. Nat. Babelon no. 360) the orientalizing Greek leaf-and-dart pattern, with pointed leaves, and the eastern lotus with rounded leaves. Hellenistic rinceaux of spirals and waves of foliage appeared on the Begram ivories but also on Gandharan reliefs, including even the small Eros-like familiars.[423]

For figures in the round there is the Buddha himself, posed now in classical contrapposto, dressed in his Indian robe rendered as a Greek himation, and with his distinctive topknot adjusted to Hellenistic modes of hairdressing [119].[424] A striking example is the Ortiz head [PL. XLI], probably 2nd-century in date, which offers even something of early Roman imperial portraiture. It

119 Statue of the Buddha.
From Mardan. 2nd cent. AD.
(After *DCAA*)

120 Relief of Hariti and Panchika under a tree. 2nd cent. AD. (London, British Museum OA 1939.1-19.18. H. 19 cm)

is from near Peshawar, and parts of its body have been identified which show that it was probably an 'acrolith', with dressed parts of the figure rendered in wood.[425] It is of a Bodhisattva, a Buddhist saint. A comparable younger head, in clay, is from Tapa Shutor [**PL. XLII**].[426] Earlier, from Mathura, a cross-legged figure seems also to boast something approximating to a classical portrait head.[427] Most Kushan royal sculpture is rendered in a strictly frontal manner that owes most to styles such as the Parthian, and partly to the steppes, but there is much also which is classicizing.

More common are smaller groups in high relief or virtually in the round, depicting deities. Figures generally identified as Panchika and Hariti, guardians of wealth and fertility, seem popular. In ill. **120** they are posed under a

121 Relief of Hariti and Panchika, seated. From Takht-I Bahi. 3rd cent. AD.
(London, British Museum OA 1950.7-26.2. H. 27.3 cm)

tree with Panchika like a near-naked Herakles, and Hariti any Greek goddess
wearing a low crown, and with the whole group reminiscent of a classical scene
of Herakles with one of the Hesperides beside the Tree of Life.[428] In ill. **121**, in
different classical poses, the god is presented more like a Dionysos and Hariti
as Tyche/Fortuna with her cornucopia.[429] The classical repertoire of figures,
dress and attributes, could, it seems, readily be adjusted to suit the presentation of Indian deities, without always one type being monopolized.[430] There

122, 123 RIGHT AND OPPOSITE Figures of Herakles/Vajrapani with thunderbolt, and Tyche/Hariti with cornucopia, flanking a Buddha at Hadda. 2nd cent. AD. (*In situ*)

124 Stone weight depicting Herakles and the lion. (New York, Metropolitan Museum.)

are also many bronze statuettes of classical deities which offer no clue as to their Indian identity, although we must assume that many had one,[431] as well as some very obvious classical origins and style.[432] Rectangular stone weights, for the use of athletes, are another Kushan genre on which classicizing motifs often appear in low relief [124].[433]

In a more monumental setting the clearest example of iconography-borrowing is probably the group at Hadda, where the Buddha is flanked by a Hellenistic Herakles [122, 123], typical for his features and pose but holding a thunderbolt, not club, so Vajrapani, and at the other side another Hariti derived directly from a classical Tyche.[434] Comparable figures and groups

125 Group of Herakles with the lion upright. (Calcutta Museum)

126 A river god. (Karachi Museum. After Ingholt)

CHAPTER 7

Greeks, Romans, Parthians and Sasanians: before Islam

We have already met the Parthians, invaders from Central Asia who took over much of Persia and the Near East after the Achaemenids had been defeated, and to whom the Seleucid Macedonians had eventually also largely given way, as they had to the new Greek kingdom in Bactria. And we have seen something of their presence in north India, as at Taxila. To the Greeks at least they could appear philhellenes. King Orodes mounted Greek plays and was said to have used the defeated Roman general Crassus' head as a prop in a production of Euripides' play *Bacchae* (Plutarch, *Crassus* 32–3). They were attacked by Romans, from sad Crassus and Mark Antony on, and usually they effectively repelled them. The Emperor Trajan took and held for a while Mesopotamia and Armenia in the early 2nd century AD, but apart from a sometimes faltering hold west and east the Parthians determined much that was built and created from the Mediterranean to Bactria, and remained in power until a new Persian dynasty, the Sasanian, claimed the old Persian heritage, one attested also by the use of Aramaic for bureaucrats. A Greek presence throughout this period is certain but Greek influence seems slight, although Parthian architecture presents many variations on – one might sometimes say travesties of – the classical, while retaining a certain oriental majesty. Thus, the details of the classical orders are copied but adjusted, and the proportions of columns can be changed out of all Mediterranean norms, from the stumpy to the elongated. More superficially Roman in appearance is the ready use of the arch, as for a moderately Roman-looking triumphal arch at Uruk [131], and the common use of acanthus ornament and Hellenistic mouldings in architecture.[443] Brick too, a Roman rather than Greek material but for far longer used in Mesopotamia, comes into its own again, notably for defence-work of Roman

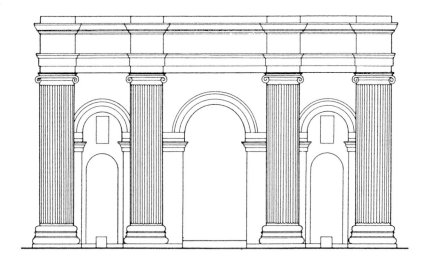

131 Triumphal arch at Uruk. 1st cent. AD.

132 Lintel with *ketea*. From Nimrud. (London, British Museum ANE 118896)

aspect.[444] Subsidiary decoration can be classical, such as acanthus leaves and floral friezes, but there is also more geometric pattern.[445] Palmyra, en route to the east, has an interesting and monumental Greco-Roman aspect.[446] For a new building at Nimrud the Greek sea monster (*ketos*) is borrowed for a lintel, and improved by being given wings and hind legs [**132**]; we have met it often in the east.[447] One cannot but think that direct Greek intervention or invention is almost wholly lacking.

For other arts, we have had occasion to wonder about a very Greek source for some of the finer Hellenistic metalwork from regions in the Parthian sphere. Otherwise, the Greek models suffer much as did the architecture, to the point that actual Greek design must be doubted. Military figures and many deities are staidly frontal, only very occasionally relaxing a pose. But as well as these there are a number of works in what one must judge a purely classical style, or one barely adjusted for somewhat unclassical figures, such as the famous bronze ruler from Shami of around the turn of the era [133].[448] At Susa there is what might be the marble portrait of a Parthian queen (Mousa?), wearing a version of the crenellated crown whose origins are both Persian and, via Cybele, Greek, and signed by a Greek artist Antiochos.[449] Of the period are also several Greek inscriptions at Susa recording manumissions, with consecration to Nanaia.[450] Divine figures get somewhat translated, notably the recliners,

133 Bronze statue from Shami. (Teheran Museum. H. 2 m)

like the Herakles/Verethagna we met at Bisitun [38]. A marble reclining lady, naked but for her necklace, is from Seleucia, offering a Greek motif in a compromise between easy classicism and blunt eastern frontality.[451] At Seleucia on the Tigris terracottas are wholly Hellenistic in form.[452] Later, in a Persian fortress site in northeast Piran (Qal'eh-i Yazdigird), we are offered stone reliefs with vine friezes, Pans, naked dancers, and Erotes with panthers [134], as plausible though not as authentic as any in the corners of the Roman Empire in the west.[453] There really is no 'common style'. Hatra is the richest source. A group presenting Allat as Athena [135] is an interesting translation of the classical,

134 Reconstructed relief with classical figures from Qaleh-I Yazdigird. (Toronto, Royal Ontario Museum 983.61.2)

135 Relief with goddesses,
showing Allat as Athena. From
Hatra. (Iraq Museum. H. 1.28 m)

136 Lintel from Hatra.
Herakles/Vajrapani reclining
at feast, with Victories.
(Iraq Museum. W. 2.5 m)

while the reclining god in ill. **136** copies the pose of the Herakles we often
meet.[454] But the last years of Hatra in the west (it was destroyed in AD 240)
yield a stiffly uncompromising sculptural style, thoroughly eastern with but a
glimpse of Roman (rather than Greek) inspiration;[455] for example, a dedication
to Herakles with one of the rare Latin inscriptions to be met in the east [**137**].
Direct Greek intervention in 'Parthian' arts is not easily defined. Certainly

there were 'Parthian' periods in Gandhara and north India – but they too are not easily defined or illustrated.

Painting traditions, on the other hand, died hard, with glimpses of the classical everywhere, but perhaps at two or three removes, and inaugurating an important period of Central Asian painting. And again, for Parthians in Central Asia, we have bronze buckles of a type well known in the area and commonly decorated with the Parthian pair of busts, but one has a very classical group of a horseman hunting a stag [138].[456]

The Sasanian kings of Persia reigned from AD 224 to 636, and their empire was no whit smaller than the Achaemenid had been; indeed it matched the Roman for the size of its army and sophistication of its defences, a feature that has been appreciated only in recent years after exploration in Central Asia.[457] It was the last and biggest of the empires of the Old World,

137 Relief from Hatra with a Latin dedication. (Iraq Museum)

138 Bronze belt plaque featuring a horseman, dog and stag. (Los Angeles County Museum)

succumbing to Islam at about the same time as did the classical Byzantine. The Sasanians devoted themselves to driving Romans out of Asia, in which they achieved no little success, with Shapur I defeating and capturing the Emperor Valerian in AD 260, a success celebrated on their own monuments in a style that owed much to the old classical traditions in the east, but with added interest in false-perspective views of the world that are pictorially very successful but owe nothing to any deliberate attempt to observe and copy the world around. In a rock relief at Naqsh-e Rustam the mounted Sasanian king grasps Valerian, at the same time receiving the homage of Emperor Philip the Arab. The same success was celebrated in a more purely classical manner on a unique cameo [**PL. XLVI**], a genre not much practised in Asia, and probably cut by a Greek.[458] The kings collide but the Persian grasps the wrist of the Roman, so he has the upper hand, and the symmetry has an eastern flavour rather than the realistic classical.

We shall return to Sasanian monumental arts, but begin with silver plate, since it is a subject already broached and in many respects it exemplifies Sasanian figurative and narrative arts. The commonest medium is the shallow silver bowl, like a phiale, followed by deeper ovoid bowls and jugs. On the bowls we find new techniques involving the soldering on of parts or all of the relief figures, and much gilding, commonly all over.[459]

We start with some problem pieces of uncertain association with the Sasanians – 'Asian' rather than 'Sasanian' – but best studied at this point in our narrative. They seem to betray a degree of remotely informed classicism that may go a little beyond the continued copying of a foreign style and figures, but which exemplifies a culture or cultures to which such a style still has a relevance, perhaps reinforced by true Greek experience, and certainly one which could offer Greek iconographic models to serve various purposes. A number of silver vessels from Central Asia betray distinct signs of classicism, without quite being Greek or even having anything very close to do with the well-known Sasanian styles. They are 'late', but how late? They are not easily dated by either their classical or eastern features, yet they clearly show knowledge of classical art and iconography. They are nearly hemispherical phialai, relief-decorated on the outside. One scholar has associated their figure decoration with knowledge of the works of the 5th-century BC Greek playwright Euripides, but the associations are probably accidental and by no means explain most of the decoration. Others place them far later, nearer the 5th century AD, which is perhaps too far and renders closer comparison with the basic Sasanian styles more difficult. All have relief roundels underneath and their rims have beading or wave pattern. The figure scenes are classical in style. On one from Kustanai (north Kazakhstan) [139] a group clearly derives from the classical formula for the scene of Admetus leaving Alcestis, but the other figures tell nothing and include a frontal seated goddess being attended. Most elements are broadly classical but only the one group specifically so. It is almost as though the artist had a pattern book of classical iconography while his style and composition are not altogether oriental in concept.

On another cup [140] there are several classical figures and groups, inviting attempts to associate them with specific scenes in classical art, but only superficially and with no common theme. On this, and another [141], a man with a club is prominent, like a Herakles but with no lionskin and belabouring another man holding a boar. The facing head in the roundel beneath looks rather like a satyr mask, and may have derived from one, but comes to have a good career in the east as the mask of the Indian war god Skanda, and called Kirtimukha. Another bowl [142], once in Tibet, has a lot of foliage and classical

139 Silver cup from Kustanai bearing groups, including one recalling the classical Admetus and Alcestis. 1st/2nd cent. AD (?). (St Petersburg, Hermitage Museum)

140 Silver cup bearing various classicizing scenes including a possible Herakles. 1st/2nd cent. AD (?). (Washington, Freer Gallery)

141 Silver cup with classicizing scenes including Herakles (?) attacking a seated man. 1st/2nd cent. AD (?). (St Petersburg, Hermitage Museum)

142 Silver bowl with figures set in a landscape of trees. From Tibet. 1st/2nd cent. AD (?). (After *DCAA*)

143 Gilt silver dish showing Herakles at feast. From Badakshan. 2nd cent. AD (?). (London, British Museum)

figures including a young Herakles with lion-head cap but no coherent narrative setting. Its base roundel has fish in water, like a dish at Begram and also on Sasanian silver,[460] and a subject for Roman mosaicists, while there are technical affinities with 'standard' Sasanian silver (the soldered-on figures).[461]

But I start with one in this technique[462] which, it is possible (indeed likely), is pre-Sasanian in date, and which carries a very remarkable and detailed copy of a totally misunderstood and reinterpreted classical motif [143]. It had been in the hands of the rulers of Badakshan (northern Pakistan) in the 19th century, acquired by the British, went to the Calcutta Museum, whence to the British

144 Sardonyx cameo showing the Triumph of Dionysos. 1st cent. BC/AD. (Naples, Museo Nazionale)

Museum, much regarded and described, although not always accurately. It is an interesting lesson in the processes of copying and interpretation, and has a very real Sasanian succession, both the whole scene and parts. However, the possibility of Parthian origin needs to be admitted, and the Parthian-Sasanian succession in silverware remains a matter for debate.[463]

The subject's origins can be readily understood from two first-century BC classical cameos showing the triumph of Dionysos.[464] On one [**144**] we see the god reclining in a chariot whose wheel is being pushed by an Eros, while another stands on the chariot pole with a torch held horizontally; the chariot is pulled by two winged women (Psychai), one of whom looks round at the other. On the other we have also an Eros flying overhead and a figure seated at the back corner of the chariot/cart. On the eastern silver dish [**143**] we have the same two women pulling the chariot with one looking round to the other, but now they have no wings and their attachment to the 'chariot' has disappeared. The flying Eros and the one on the chariot pole keep their postures but are now joined by a ribbon and one Eros holds a jug. The chariot has become a plain rectangle, which is the way carpets are soon to be shown in the east and may be so translated already here. Its wheel is still being attended to by an Eros and there is a female figure seated at one corner, as on the cameos. The reclining figure holding a bowl is no longer Dionysos but the Herakles type

recall the Dioskouroi at Dilberzin [46], but, with the horses winged and with bent heads, certainly also evoking something of the popular classical motif of Bellerophon watering Pegasus on Acrocorinth, especially since there seems to be a water-carrier below them, presenting a fine confusion of myth and iconography.[475] The winged horses appear alone also in Sasanian art and they are shown beside royal thrones.[476] It is not clear whether the partly clothed men and festive near-naked women, some with vines and Pan pipes, which are prominent on Sasanian plate are indeed lingering shadows of Dionysos and his maenads [149].[477] They may indeed owe something to classical models, yet seem almost an integral part of Sasanian court imagery, but even the Roman wolf with Romulus and Remus has an eastern currency.[478]

Sasanian seal engravings offer a very wide range of subjects, a few of which are classically inspired. On one [150] we see a Sasanian hero dealing with what

149 Sasanian gilt silver flask showing a woman piping in a vineyard. 3rd cent. AD (?). (Washington, Freer Gallery)

looks very much like the Greek god Pan, ithyphallic and with animal extremities.[479] Pan himself is not so treated in the west but his figure was widely used, including in Parthia, to personify any rustic demon.

In Sasanian architecture the remnants of classicism are more disguised but the Corinthian order is remembered in capitals of the same general shape, without the flowing leaves, but with a fine mix of classicizing florals in low relief [151].[480] This is in fact a type also widespread in the eastern Byzantine Empire and later will be found from Córdoba in Spain to Faras in Nubia.[481]

150 Sasanian medallion with a ruler attacking a Pan-like figure. (Paris, Bibliothèque Nationale 1975.251.12)

151 Sasanian 'Corinthian' capital from Taq-I Bustan. 4th/5th cent. AD (?). (Photo, author)

More unusual and thought-provoking is the possibility that Sasanian art contributed to the western iconography of episodes in the 'Alexander Romance', a colourful account of Alexander's further exploration of the world in an animal-powered flying machine. There are Sasanian representations of the raising of the Moon God, and of rulers on thrones that seem about to take off, lifted by winged monsters, as in ill. **146**.[482] The subject was one which was current in much later Persian art.

The Sasanians, although generally successful against the Romans, met their match in the Emperor Heraclius, who, in the early 7th century, drove their armies deep back into Persia. But very soon after, both his, that is the Eastern Roman Empire, and the Sasanian Empire, fell to the advance of Islam.

Epilogue: myth, history and archaeology

> By founding more than seventy cities among the barbarian tribes and
> sowing Asia with Greek magistrates Alexander conquered its undomes-
> ticated and beastly way of life.
>
> Plutarch, *Moralia* 328e

> Alexander persuaded the Sogdians to support their parents, not to kill
> them, and the Persians to respect their mothers, not to marry them....
> A most admirable philosophy, which induced the Indians to worship
> Greek gods, and the Scythians to bury their dead and not to eat them.
>
> Plutarch, *de Alexandri Magni Fortuna aut Virtute* 1.328c

We can never quite get away from the Greeks' high opinion of themselves,
what they thought they had brought to the rest of the world – 'barbarian'
because it talked 'bar-bar-bar' and not Greek – and how much it owed them.
And their own history obliged many of them to pretend that Alexander was
really a Greek who pursued Greek moral aims. Strabo was, uncharacteristi-
cally, more honest about Greek influence in the east: 'we regard the Scythians
as the most straightforward of men and the least prone to mischief, as also far
more frugal and independent of others than we are. And yet our mode of life
has spread its change for the worse to almost all peoples, introducing among
them luxury and sensual pleasures, and, to satisfy these vices, base artifices
that lead to innumerable acts of greed. So then, much wickedness of this sort
has fallen on barbarian peoples also, on the nomads as the rest' (Strabo 301).

In this epilogue I want first to consider briefly what role Greek myth-making took in their recreation of history, since it was very real to the main actors
in our story and they took their gods and heroes seriously. We saw in Chapter 2
what a Homer might make of conflict and contact with easterners in the
Bronze Age (see pp. 50–51), but Homer is exceptional in succeeding to bring
into his narrative both real royal families and the families of gods and heroes,

interacting in the interests of the Greek people, even if not of all of them, all of the time. And he is composing and writing four or five hundred years after the 'events', drawing on oral traditions about both history and myth which must have been very flexible, and involving a deliberate Greek invention of an 'Age of Heroes'. It is easy to overestimate the degree to which he was influenced by eastern models of stories of gods and humans. There are some very telling parallels with eastern myth-history but for the most part the parallels are slight or even accidental. The ancient world was not as big as we might think, and there was good if not full awareness of how foreign neighbours behaved and how their poets entertained them and recorded the 'history' of their kings and gods.

More than most ancient peoples, it seems, the Greeks lived with their gods and heroes embedded not only in their religious practices, but in their politics and everyday life, without being dominated by priestly classes serving despotic rulers. This flexibility allowed much local invention to explain both natural and political issues. The ready equation of a prominent mortal with a hero was but one aspect of this. When the 'tyrant' Peisistratos marched on Athens in the mid-6th century BC he travelled in a chariot accompanied by a woman dressed as the goddess Athena – more than adequate credentials, and using a chariot as a processional vehicle rather than aggressively (the Greeks of the day did not fight from chariots).[483]

Going east, the Greeks in the Black Sea area soon accommodated their experience of steppe warriors to their own view of the possibility and behaviour of warrior-women in the east – the Amazons – no little helped by the fact that nomad women could fight beside their menfolk, and maybe by the common lack of facial hair among Asiatics.[484] There was even a late story of Alexander meeting Amazons.[485] For the monsters that guarded the gold sought by the Arimasps they had their own version of the griffin monster.[486] The Black Sea coast became a setting for Greek myth – Iphigeneia becoming a priestess in the Crimea before being rescued by Orestes, Jason mounting a whole expedition to Colchis (Georgia) to win both the golden fleece (how gold was got from the rivers of the Caucasus) and Medea. Odysseus' travels as told by Homer are full of mythical dilemmas but seem really to chart exploration of various western waters in the days of colonization.

In Asia Minor old Hittite monuments could give rise to stories of mythical thrones, even a Niobe turned to stone.[487] Cyprus was rich ground since Greeks had been active there since the end of the Bronze Age, and it was easy to place the birth of a very oriental goddess like Aphrodite on, or just off, the island. The Greeks colonized not only the lands where they settled but also those they had simply visited or heard about with their mythological nexus, abetted by the skills of artists and poets whose works seemed very accessible at all levels of society. Myth scenes are commonplace on everyday objects, and the stories and even lines of the plays staged in Athens became common property; soldiers who had perhaps sung in the chorus in Athens could regale their captive mates in Sicily with recitals of Euripides.

The Caucasus was where Zeus had staked out Prometheus, a punishment for stealing fire for man, and where Herakles rescued him from the daily attentions of Zeus' eagle tearing out his (immortal) liver. A locale was no doubt pointed out, but so it was also for the same episode yet farther east, in the Hindu Kush,[488] and we are faced with Greek myth-making intruding into areas which have been our concern in the chapters above. The Greek world was circumscribed by an 'Ocean' allowing no knowledge of what lay beyond, but real Greeks had already, perforce, crossed that barrier, and Herodotus' knowledge of what lay beyond was more than mere hearsay. Greeks captured by Persians had been humanely resettled by their captors in Bactria, a country not so unlike Greece, even in its suitability for viniculture. This is probably why at the end of the 5th century Euripides knew of Bactria as the place whence the god Dionysos had come, to wreak his vengeance on poor Pentheus in Thebes. Dionysos, as god of wine, could readily be accommodated in the east, and he was exceptional in the Greek pantheon for his universal interests. Soon (about 400 BC) a quite persianized Dionysos could appear in Greek art [152], mounted on a camel, attended by his maenads and Persian dancers.[489]

Dionysos was an important figure in the east. He was held to have conquered the world, persuading mankind about the values of wine, and to have been particularly successful with the Indians. Local associations were found, as we have seen; and 'the habit of the Indians to go to battle to the sound of drums and cymbals and in dappled costumes' (Arrian, *Indica* 5.9–10). The figure of the god himself does not appear much in the east rather than many other figures and scenes, maenadic rather than of satyrs, and there is much broadly Dionysiac imagery and decoration. The contrast with Herakles is interesting. The latter's image could be used for an eastern deity or hero, Persian Verethagna or Indian Vajrapani, and was otherwise also very common in varieties of his usual classical form all over the area we have discussed, even without any obvious associations with local gods.

The appearance in art and worship of other Greek gods was a matter for the Indo-Greek states and conducted much as it had been at home together with the traditional imagery, notably on coins, where, however, local considerations could promote some original iconography. Aphrodite and figures related to her would certainly have helped inform both images and behaviour, such

152 Athenian red-figure vase showing Dionysos in Persian dress riding a Bactrian camel. Accompanied by dancing Persians and women with tambourine and fan. About 400 BC. (London, British Museum E 695. After Furtwängler)

as we have seen in the Indian adoption of the more exotic and flimsy styles of Hellenistic jewelry as a substitute for dress. Nudity was no novelty in eastern art; however, total physical realism certainly was, such as that which is peculiar to Greek art from the mid-5th century on, and unlike the treatment of figures in any other of the early arts of the urban world. Aphrodite may have derived much from comparable eastern figures, like Astarte, but the oriental sex goddesses were never allowed to look seductive with such fully realistic treatment – nor were other human figures, unless they were clearly the creations of Greek artists. It was something that the rest of the world remained blind to or deliberately shunned.[490]

At the end of the last chapter I remarked on the possibility that Sasanian art contributed to western depictions of the Alexander Romance. It may not be inapposite to remark that the east's interest in western subjects and arts did not stop with the advent of Islam. The Persians were ready enough to adopt Alexander stories ('Iskander' to them) in their arts and there are fine paintings of Alexander on his campaigns as well as in his romantic adventures. The relationship did not end with antiquity. In Shah Jahan's 17th-century Red Throne room at Delhi there were Italian *pietra dura* plaques depicting the story of Orpheus, charming wild animals with his music.[491] The theme had appeared in Persian art earlier, where a ruler might be shown in the peaceful company of wild animals, yet the classical iconography of Orpheus seems not to have carried east in earlier centuries. We do find, however, a Renaissance bronze plaque with the theme, dated *c.* AD 1600 or later, from Afghanistan (**153**).[492] The classicism of the Renaissance seems to offer an unexpected coda to our story of Mediterranean arts, stories and peoples in Asia.

153 Netherlandish bronze plaque showing Orpheus charming the wild animals. From Afghanistan. About AD 1600. (Oxford, Ashmolean Museum EA 1995.3)

Abbreviations

ACSS: *Ancient Civilizations from Scythia to Siberia*.

Afghanistan (New York): *Afghanistan. Forging Civilizations along the Silk Road* (New York, Metropolitan Museum, 2012).

After Alexander: J. Cribb & G. Herrmann (eds), *After Alexander* (Oxford, 2007).

AWE: *Ancient West and East*.

BAI: *Bulletin of the Asia Institute*.

Ball 2000: W. Ball, *Rome in the East* (London, 2000).

Ball 2008: W. Ball, *The Monuments of Afghanistan* (London, 2008).

Ball, *Persia*: W. Ball, *Towards One World: Ancient Persia and the West* (London, 2010).

Boardman, *GSLCP*: J. Boardman, *Greek Sculpture, the Late Classical Period* (1995).

Boardman, *GGFR*: J. Boardman, *Greek Gems and Finger Rings* (London, 1979, 2001); and see *DCAA, PW, TTG*.

Boardman, *GO*: J. Boardman, *The Greeks Overseas* (1999).

Bosworth, *Arrian*: A. B. Bosworth, *A Historical Commentary on Arrian's History of Alexander* I, II (1980, 1995).

Bosworth, *Alexander*: A. B. Bosworth, *Alexander and the East: the Tragedy of Triumph* (1996).

Brunt, *Arrian*: P. A. Brunt, *Arrian: History of Alexander and Indica* (Loeb, 1989).

CAH: *Cambridge Ancient History*.

CII: *Corpus Inscriptionum Iranicarum* II (London, 2012) by G. Rougemont et al.

Colledge, *Parthians*: M. A. R. Colledge, *The Parthians* (London, 1967).

Crossroads: E. Errington & J. Cribb (eds), *The Crossroads of Asia* (Cambridge, 1992).

Czuma 1985: S. J. Czuma, *Kushan Sculpture Images from India* (Cleveland Museum, 1985).

DCAA: J. Boardman, *The Diffusion of Classical Art in Antiquity* (1994).

Errington: E. Errington, London thesis (1987) on Jamalgarhi (British Library).

Ettinghausen, *BSI*: R. Ettinghausen, *From Byzantium to Sasanian Iran and the Islamic World* (Leiden, 1972).

Francfort: Henri-Paul Francfort, *Les Palettes du Gandhara* (Mem. Del. Arch. Fr. 23, 1979).

Frankfort 1996: H. Frankfort, *The Art and Architecture of the Ancient Orient* (1996).

Fraser, *Cities*: P. M. Fraser, *Cities of Alexander the Great* (1996).

GAC: R. Allchin, B. Allchin, N. Kreitman & E. Errington (eds), *Gandharan Art in Context* (New Delhi, 1997).

Galli 2011: M. Galli, 'Hellenistic Court Imagery in the Early Buddhist Art of Gandhara': *ACSS* 17, 279–329.

Gandhara: *From Pella to Gandhara* (Oxford, BAR 2221, 2011) – 2008 conference.

GSEM: G. Tsetskhladze & A. M. Snodgrass (eds), *Greek Settlements in the Eastern Mediterranean and the Black Sea* (BAR, 2002).

Harle 1986: J. C. Harle, *The Art and Architecture of the Indian Subcontinent* (Penguin Books).

Herrmann 1977: G. Herrmann, *The Iranian Revival* (London, 1977).

Holt, *Lost World*: F. L. Holt, *Lost World of the Golden King* (Univ. California, 2012).

Ingholt: H. Ingholt, *Gandharan Art in Pakistan* (New York, 1957).

IAW: G. Pollet (ed.), *India and the Ancient World. History Trade and Culture before* AD *650* (Eggermont Jubilee Volume; Leuven, 1987).

JIAAA: *Journal of Inner Asian Art and Archaeology*.

Lane Fox 1986: R. Lane Fox, *Alexander the Great* (1986).

Litvinsky Festschrift: V. Valsina et al. (eds), *Tsentralnaya Asiya* (Moscow, 2005).

Lotus: M. Lerner & S. Kossak, *The Lotus Transcendent* (New York, 1991).

Lukonin: V. G. Lukonin, *Persia* II (Geneva, Archaeologia Mundi, 1967).

Lydian Treasure: I. Ozgen & J. Ozturk, *Heritage recovered. The Lydian Treasure* (Ministry of Culture, Ankara, 1996).

Mairs 2011, 2013: R. Mairs, *The Archaeology of the Hellenistic Far East. A Survey* (Oxford, BAR 2196, 2011); and Supplement 1 (Feb. 2013; www.bactria.org).

Mayor, *Mithradates*: A. Mayor, *The Poison King, the life and legend of Mithradates* (Princeton, 2010).

MGB: O. Bopearachchi, *Monnaies greco-bactriennes et indo-grecques* (Paris, 1991).

Mordvintseva, *Sarmatische Phaleren* (Rahden, 2001).

Narain, *Indo-Greeks*: A. K. Narain, *The Indo-Greeks* (Oxford 1957); and cf. his ch. 11 in *CAH* VIII (1989).

Nehru, *OGS*: L. Nehru, *The Origins of Gandhara Sculpture* (Oxford University Press, Delhi, 1989).

Oxus: *Oxus, neue Funde aus der Sowjetrepublik Tadschikistan* (Museum Rietburg, Zurich, 1989).

PW: J. Boardman, *Persia and the West* (2000).

RA: *Revue Archéologique*.

Rahman Dar 1984: S. Saifur Rahman Dar, *Taxila and the Western World* (Lahore, 1984).

Rowland 1977: B. Rowland, *The Art and Architecture of India* (Penguin Books, 1977 – revised by J. C. Harle).

SAS: *South Asian Studies*.

SAA: *South Asian Archaeology*.

Sherwin-White/Kuhrt 1993: S. Sherwin-White & A. Kuhrt, *From Samarkhand to Sardis* (1993).

SRAA: *Silk Road Art and Archaeology*.

Susa: J. Perrot (ed.), *Susa* (London, 2013).

Tarn, *Bactria and India*: W. W. Tarn, *The Greeks in Bactria and India* (1st ed. 1938; 3rd ed. with revisions by F. L. Holt, Chicago 1997).

TT: V. Sarianidi, *The Golden Hoard of Bactria* (Leningrad, 1985); there are different editions in English, and in other languages, with the same figure numeration.

TTG: J. Boardman, 'The Tillya Tepe Gold: a closer look' in *AWE* 2 (2003) 48–74.

Notes

1   S. Amigues, *Journal des Savants* 2011, 71.

2   Their earliest home remains a matter for speculation but it seems that their language retained elements in common with Phrygian and Armenian in east Asia Minor: C. de Lamberterie, *J. des Savants* (2013) 3–69.

3   This is not the message of C. Renfrew, *The Emergence of Civilisation* (1973) which is mainly based on periods when there is no evidence beyond archaeology. I make it a major element in my *The World of Ancient Art* (2006).

4   Boardman, *GO* 272–8; 'Aspects of Colonization' in *Bull.Amer.Sch.Or.Res.* 322 (2001) 33–42.

5   Also on the advice and help of others, notably Lolita Nehru, Warwick Ball, Osmund Bopearachchi, Claudia Wagner.

6   D.F. Graf, 'The Persian Royal Road System' in *Achaemenid History* VIII (eds A. Kuhrt et al., 1995) 167–89.

7   On the emergence of the Silk Roads see Y. Juping in *The Silk Road* 6.2 (2009) 15–22.

8   See, notably, for our area, his *Between Oxus and Jumna* (1961), and throughout his last book *Mankind and Mother Earth* (1976).

9   *GAC* 1.

Chapter 1

10   For a very broad view of the Bronze Age to archaic period in Greece, J. Boardman, *Preclassical* (1967).

11   P.T. Daniels and W. Bright, *The World's Writing Systems* (New York, 1996), esp. Daniels, 23–8.

12   For this see my *GO*, also for the Euboeans in the west (and in *OJA* 25 (2006) 195–200 for the Carthage area); and Boardman in *GSEM* 1–16. On Euboeans in general and their explorations in this period R.L. Fox, *Travelling Heroes* (2008). For the eastern cultures, Frankfort 1996, and in general also W. Burkert, *The Orientalizing Revolution* (1992).

13   J. Boardman in *Greek Settlements in the East Mediterranean and the Black Sea* (eds G. Tsetskhladze, A.M. Snodgrass, Oxford, BAR, 2002) 8–10.

14   For the reactionary view about Greek Geometric pottery going east simply for its appearance see J.N. Coldstream in *AWE* 8 (2009) 21–36

15   Boardman, *GO* 51, 272.

16   *GO* 35–51 deals with the Greeks in the east in the 8th to 6th century in detail.

17   R. Rollinger in *Companion to the Classical World* (ed. K.H. Kinzl, 2006) 197–226; and in *State Archives of Assyria Bulletin* 16 (2007) 63–90. G. Töttössy in *Acta Antiqua* 3 (1955) 301ff. on the name for the Greeks in ancient India.

18   J. Boardman, *OJA* 25 (2006) 195–200, on early Greek exploration of the Carthage area, indicated by place names.

19   See on Crete *GO* 58–61; J. Boardman, *The Cretan Collection in Oxford* (Oxford, 1961) ch. 5.

20   J. Boardman, *The Archaeology of Nostalgia* (2002) 106–7.

21   *GO* 30, fig. 4; 97, fig. 110, a section through the walls and siege-mound.

22   A. Fantalkin, 'Naucratis as a contact zone' in *Colloquia Antiqua* 10 (Kulturkontakten in antiken Welten, eds R. Rollinger, K. Schnegg, 2009) 27–51.

23   *GO* 257, fig. 298; ivory figure of a boar.

24   Samos has early material suggesting links with the Caucasus and the Black Sea, *GO* 64–5.

25   *DCAA* 197f., fig. 6.14. GO 260, fig. 303; and compare the rhyton, fig. 304

26   *BCH Supplement* 14 (1986; *Iconographie Classique*) 275, fig. 2 (V. Schiltz). On the Rolltier see B. Brentjes, *Arch.Mitt.Iran* 27 (1994) 147–64.

27 See *DCAA* ch. 6; *GO* ch. 6.

28 *DCAA* 201–2, figs. 6.21 (dentistry), 23.

29 Ibid., 215, fig. 6.43; cf. 209, fig. 6.32.

30 Ibid., 210, figs. 6.35–6.

31 J. Boardman in *Afghanistan* (New York, 2012) 108, fig. 7.

32 *DCAA* 217–22, the plaque, 219, fig. 6.46.

33 On fish in the Mediterranean and salt see J. Boardman, *AWE* 10 (2011) 1–9. The only export on Greek ships recorded leaving Egypt in 475 BC was natron salt, for pickling; see J. Boardman, *AWE* 12 (2013) 265–7.

Chapter 2

34 Ball, *Persia*, gives and excellent account of Persian fortunes in the Greek and Roman periods; and notably 31–8 on Greeks outside Europe and Ionia. And for the literary associations, J. Haubold, *Greece and Mesopotamia. Dialogues in literature* (Cambridge, 2012).

35 On early cruelty see J. Boardman in *Amymona Erga* (Fest. V. Lambrinoudakis, 2007) 257–64.

36 M. Brosius, *Women in Ancient Persia* (Oxford, 1996).

37 On Zoroastrianism in the east Ball 2000, 433–8.

38 H.J. Kim, *Ethnicity and Foreigners in Ancient Greece and China* (Duckworth, 2009).

39 An excellent account of Anatolia in this period is E. Dusinberre, *Empire, Authority, and Autonomy in Achaemenid Anatolia* (Cambridge, 2013). And cf. C.H. Rodenwaldt, *The Archaeology of Lydia from Gyges to Alexander* (Cambridge, 2009).

40 *Lydian Treasure* no. 78. On Lydian/Achaemenid silver, A. Melikian-Chirvani, *Bull.As.Inst.* 7 (1993) 111–30

41 E.g., *DCAA* 43, fig. 2.31, a gilt silver vase handle in the form of a winged ibex.

42 An unusual and very early instance being on the Median scabbard (from the Oxus Treasure but made farther to the west). J. Boardman in *Litvinsky Festschrift* 205–14, and *Iran* 44 (2006) 115–9.

43 On the pyramidal stamps seals see J. Boardman, *Iran* 8 (1970) 1–45 (PL. 2.23–4 = [fig. 9]); 36 (1998) 1–13.

44 On Greco-Persian seals see Boardman, *GGFR* ch. 6; *PW* 152–174. The pieces illustrated are *GGFR* PLS. 880 [fig. 10], 856 [fig. 11], 910, 901 [fig. 12]; *PW* fig. 5.44 [fig. 13]. A splendid tabloid with a Persian horseman spearing a Greek horseman was on the Kabul market in 1972: H. Francfort, *Journal Asiatique* 263 (1975) 219–22.

45 *PW* 174–8, for the pieces illustrated.

46 British Museum. Boardman, *GSLCP* fig. 218.11.

47 *DCAA* 40–1, fig. 2.27, from Elmali. E. Akurgal, *The Birth of Greek Art* (London, 1966) PL. 68, from Duver.

48 *DCAA* 41, fig. 2.28.

49 Boardman, *GSLCP* figs. 208–17; fig. 219, the Hellenistic.

50 B.F. Cook, *Relief Sculptures of the Mausoleum at Halicarnassus* (Oxford, 2005); Boardman, *GSLCP* 27–9.

51 Dusinberre, op. cit., 57–9; ch. 5 for tomb design.

52 Fantalkin, op. cit., n. 22.

53 In general on this orientalized Greekness see M. Munn, *The Mother of Gods. Athens and the tyranny of Asia* (Berkeley, 2006).

54 H. Gitler and O. Tal, *Israel Numismatic Research* 7 (2012) 7–15.

55 *DCAA* 54–5; *GSLCP* fig. 225.

56 J. Boardman, *The Archaeology of Nostalgia* (London, 2002) 54, fig. 23.

57 *PW* 182, fig. 5.63 (the shield). For the relevant sarcophagi and sculptures of Anatolia and Phoenicia see chs. 11, 12 in Boardman, *GSLCP*.

58 C. Nylander, in *Architetti, Capomastri, Artigiani; Studi, D. Facenna* (2006) 134, fig. 11, 'I am Pytharchos'. *CII* nos. 55–57. In later, Seleucid Persepolis, there are Greek dedications on altars for Greek gods, ibid., nos. 59–63.

59 Greeks in Persepolis, Boardman, *PW* 131–4, figs. 4.3–5.

60 Boardman, *PW* 53–9.

61 Ibid., 64.

62 Ibid., 102–4.

63 Ibid., 128–31.

64 Well described and illustrated now in J. Perrot (ed.), *Susa* (London, 2013).

65 The architectural borrowings and adaptations are dealt with thoroughly in Boardman, *PW*; the Darius figure [fig. 25], pp. 114–6, the Susa soldiers, 112, fig. 3.33 [PL. V]. See also C. Nylander, *Ionians at Pasargadae* (Uppsala 1970).

66 T.S. Kawami, *Monumental Architecture of the Parthian Period in Iran* (1987) PL. 20.

67 Boardman, *PW* 111, fig. 3.32; O. Palagia in *Ancient Greece and Ancient Iran* (eds S.M.R. Darbandi, A. Zournatzi, Athens, 2008) 223–37.

68 Boardman, *PW* 136–7; Perrot, op. cit. fig. 394 (siren rhyton).

69 *PW* 199, fig. 5.83.

70 On these matters see M.C. Miller, *Athens and Persia in the Fifth Century* BC (1997); J. Boardman, 'Persia in Europe' in *Colloquia Antiqua* I (2011)

Greeks West and East (ed. G. Tsetskhladze, 1999) 565–604, and Mordvintseva. Pfrommer, op. cit. (n. 10).

202 *DCAA* , fig. 4.40.; St Petersburg. P. Goukowsky in *BCH* 96 (1972) 473–502 for the Greek turret.

203 J. Boardman 'The Ketos in India' in *BCH* Suppl. XIV (1986) 447–53 (where the plural is misspelled *ketoi*); 'Very like a whale' in *Monsters and Demons in the ancient and mediaeval worlds* (ed. E. Porada, Mainz, 1987) 73–84.

204 *DCAA* 107, fig. 4.40; St Petersburg; from between Omsk and Tobolsk.

205 Mordvintseva no. 36. M. Treister, *ACSS* 18 (2014) 81–109.

206 Mordvintseva, no. 43.

207 *Archeo* 21.4 (242) *Sarmati* 65, fig.

208 Still best expounded in E. Minns, *Scythians and Greeks* (Cambridge, 1913) and see V. Schiltz, *Die Skythen* (Munich 1994).

209 The griffin in Indian art, M. Magistro, *Parthica* 1 (1999) 171–95.

210 For the Altai finds see S. Rudenko, *The Culture of the population of the High Altai in the Scythian Period* (Moscow/Leningrad, 1953).

211 K. Abdullaev, *CRAI* 2007, 562–3, fig. 16; *Parthica* 10 (2008) 135–49.

212 M. Wagner et al., 'The Ornamental trousers from Sampula', *Antiquity* 83 (2009) 1067, fig. 2a. E. Knauer, *The Camel's Load* (2011) 110, fig. 75.

213 In *AWE* 11 (2012) 134–8, I suggest that the Issyk-Kul 'Golden Man' burial might be of a Yuehzhi going west, not an earlier Scythian chief. J.F. Haskins, *BAI* 2 (1988) 1–10, thinks that the Massagetai in Greek sources are the migrant Yuehzhi. For the finds, see now *Nomads and Networks* (eds S. Stark and K.S. Rubinson, New York, 2012). For Ferghana, E. Gorbunova, *The Culture of Ancient Ferghana* (Oxford, BAR 281, 1986). On the Yuehzhi, their Tocharian language and history, there are important essays in *The Bronze Age and Early Iron Age Peoples of Eastern Central Asia* (ed. V.M. Mair, Washington, 1998). C. Benjamin in *Eran and Aneran* (Fest. B. Marshak, 2003) on the Yuehzhi in Sogdia.

214 The neatest account of his mission is in Tarn, esp. 119–22, 295–9.

215 B.J. Staviskij, *La Bactriane sous les Kushans* (1986) is somewhat dated but a useful guide to sites.

216 I study the Greek elements at Tillya Tepe in *AWE* 2 (2003) 348–74 (here *TTG*); and further in *Afghanistan* (ed. J. Aruz, New York, 2012) 102–11. There has been much discussion of the finds in recent years thanks to the travelling exhibition and a tendency by some to explain the complex as more nomad than Yuehzhi, but the finds tell their own story and only the Yuehzhi and the local early history of the area can explain the variety of sources and influences. Sarianidi found some Bronze Age elements in the work of the Tillya Tepe goldsmiths: *Sov.Arch.* 1987.1, 77–83. On local sources for gold see Holt, *Lost World* 163–4. Gold nuggets could be found in the Oxus: Aristotle, *Mir.* 46

217 On the coins at Tillya Tepe see also Holt, *Lost World* 197–8.

218 Other coins at Tillya Tepe include a Roman coin of the Emperor Tiberius, and an obol of Hermaios.

219 Burial 6.4; *TT* figs. 48–50; *TTG* fig. 11.

220 Burial 6.3, *TT* fig. 99; *TTG* fig. 14.

221 Burial 6.2; *TTG* fig 1.

222 See J. Boardman, *The Triumph of Dionysos* (Oxford BAR, 2014).

223 Burial 2.6; *TT* fig. 80; *TTG* fig. 13.

224 Burial 3.51; *TT* figs. 18,19.

225 Burial 3.1; *TT* figs. 81–4; *TTG* fig. 4.

226 On the echoes of Greek armour in the east, see E. R. Knauer, 'Knemides in the East?' in *Nomodeiktes* (Studies in honour of Martin Oswald, Ann Arbor, 1993) 235–54. On defensive armour in Asia, A.E. Dien, *Journal of East Asian Archaeology* 2,3/4 (2000) 1–22.

227 Burial 4.1; *TT* figs. 88–97; *TTG* fig. 3. See also S. Peterson, *Parthian Aspects of Objects from Grave IV, T.T.*

228 On Nana, M. Ghose, *JIAAA* 1 (2006) 97–112; K. Abdullaev in *SRAA* 9 (2003) 15–38.

229 For such a sleeve restored see *Scythian Gold* (ed. E.D. Reeder, 1999) 27, fig. 3. In general on nomad dress see E.R. Knauer in *CRAI* 1999, 1141–87.

230 Burial 1.1; *TT* fig. 86; *TTG* fig. 7.

231 *TTG* fig. 8, and for discussion of the associations; *BCH* Suppl. 29 (1996) PL. 93.2,3,

232 I discuss these in detail in *Relief Plaques of Eastern Eurasia and China* (Oxford, Beazley Archive, 2010), supplemented in *AWE* 11 (1912) 123–45.

233 *Relief Plaques...*, 69, PLS. colour 3.310; 42.310.

234 On the *ketos* in the east see above, n. 203.

235 See *After Alexander* 20–24. In fig. 64 the left pair are Chinese, the right pair Greek, the lower one from Tillya Tepe.

236 U. Hermberg, *Gewürze, Weihrauch, Seide:Welthandel in der Antike* (1971) 39. The carnelian beads that appear in early China need

not have come from far to the west, though likely to be of western Asian origin: J. Rawson, 'Carnelian Beads, Animal Figures and Exotic Vessels', *Archeologie in China* 1, *Bridging Eurasia* (2010) 1–42. S. Lieberman, *Contacts between Rome and China* (Michigan thesis 1953) 203–30 lists finds, notably coins. Ball 2000, 133–9 on Rome and China. For classical gems in the Thai-Malay peninsula, B. Borell et al., in N. Revire, *Before Siam* (2013) 99–117 (fig. 1 is a rare piece of cameo glass).

237   Dr Ian Glover told me of this.

238   *J. Malayan Branch Royal As. Soc.* 26.2 (1953) 64.

239   J. Rawson in *Pots and Pans* (Oxford Studies in Islamic Art III. 1986, ed. M. Vickers), 32–3, fig. 1.

240   J. Rawson, *Chinese Ornament* (BM, 1984) 40, fig. 15

241   *China Archaeology and Art Digest* 1.2 (1996) 279. F. Barratte, *Arts Asiatiques* 51 (1996) 142–7.

242   M. Rostovtseff, *L'Art Gréco-Sarmate et l'Art Chinois* (*Arethuse* April 1924.3) PL. 17.3 (Louvre).

243   *China: Dawn of a Golden Age 200–750 AD* (ed. C.Y. Watt, New York, 2004) no. 157; with what seem to be a Judgement of Paris, Helen abducted, Helen with Menelaus.

244   See Arts (below, n. 250).

245   *Crossroads* no. 95; *DCAA* 149, fig. 4.95. On such bronze vessels in Central Asia, B. Litvinski, *East and West* 52 (2002) 127–149.

246   *DCAA* 149, fig. 4.96. On Phrygian helmets, I. Vokotopoulou, *AA* 1982, 497–520. For the helmet type in the east see A.S. Balachvantsev in *Litvinsky Festschrift* 176–7.

247   *DCAA* 150–3, figs. 4.97–102. In *DCAA* there is a far more fully documented account of such echoes of the west in the east. For the helmet type in the east see A.S. Balachvantsev in *Litvinsky Festschrift* 176–7.

248   It seems likely that the early discoveries of silk in Europe need have nothing to do with China: I. Good, 'On the Question of Silk in pre-Han Eurasia', *Antiquity* 69 (1995) 959–68. Also E.R. Knauer, *The Camels' Load in Life and Death* (Kilchberg, 2011) 30–3, in detail. Some Chinese Han mirrors in Europe: V. Guguev et al., *Bull.of the Metals Museum* 16 (1991) 32–50.

249   On caravan-cities F. Millar, *Bull.Inst.Class.Stud.* 42 (1998) 119–37.

250   There is a good summary of these contacts and later influences farther east in P.L.W. Arts, *Violets between Cherry Blossoms* (The Diffusion of Classical Motifs to the East. Traces in Japanese Arts; London 2011) 110–36.

251   *Treasures of Ancient Bactria* (Miho, 2002) no. 214.

252   L. Nikel, *Bull.Amer.School Oriental and African Studies* 76 (2013) 413–47.

253   Lane Fox 1986, 370–1.

254   Cf. J. Boardman, *The World of Ancient Art* (2006) PLS. 79–97 (Chinese stylization), 98, 105 (realistic painting), 101 (the terracotta army); 4–5 (palaeolithic realism), 536 (Peru).

Chapter 6

255   G.L. Possehl, 'Indus-Mesopotamian Trade', *Iranica Antiqua* 37 (2002) 325–42.

256   An important essay on this by G.M. Bongard-Levin is 'Ancient India and the Greco-Roman World' in *Indologica Taurinensia* 13 (1985–6) 169–85. Generally, on the Greeks' views on Indians see Lane Fox 1986, 347–9, and ch. 33.

257   Cf. A.B. Bosworth in *Classical Philology* 91 (1996) 113–27.

258   *Camb.Hist.Class.Literature* I (1985) 657.

259   J. Boardman, *The Archaeology of Nostalgia* (2002) 41–2, and for the griffins, 127–32, also noted by Ctesias.

260   Bongard-Levin, op. cit., 178–83. Various Greek words, of significant meaning, were adopted: *mela* for ink; *kalamo* for pen; *khlania* for bridle; *barbara* (see article by Sanujit atwww.ancient.eu.com/article/208/).

261   V. Dehejia, 'On modes of visual narration in early Buddhist art', *Art Bulletin* 72 (1990) 374–92. An excellent survey of the arts of India in Harle 1986, whose predecessor in the Pelican series, Rowland 1977, is somewhat fuller on the early period.

262   V.-P. Yailenko, 'Les maximes delphiques d'Ai Khanoum et la formation de la doctrine du *dhamma* d'Asoka', in *DHA* 1990, 239–56.

263   *DCAA* 331, n. 85. J. Irwin, articles on the pillars in *Burlington Magazine* 1973, 1974, 1975, 1976; especially for the florals. Rowland 1977, 68–9.

264   *DCAA* 110, fig. 4.41. N.G. Majumbar, *Guide to the Sculptures of the India Museum* (Calcutta) I, PL. 1b; PL. 1a is similar with a single seated lion and frieze of birds.

265   *DCAA* 110, fig. 4.42. And see J. Irwin in *IAW* 87–93 on their lack of bases and restorations, and ibid., 131–9, K.R. Norman on the inscribing.

266   *DCAA* 113, fig. 4.44. There seems evidence that masons at Bharhut came from Gandhara; ibid., 331, n. 103. A comprehensive account of Bharhut and its sculpture in A. C. Coomaraswamy, *La Sculpture de Bharhut* (1956).

267 *DCAA* 113, fig. 4.45.

268 Ibid., 114, fig. 4.46.

269 Ibid., 151–3.

270 J. Boardman, 'Reflections on the Origins of Indian stone architecture' in *BAI* 12 (1998) 13–22, for more detail. On Greek bead-and-reel in India, R. Morton-Smith in *East and West* 25 (1975) 439–51.

271 E.g. from Mathura, Czuma 1985, nos. 8, 9.

272 Cf. Ball 2000, 281. For an entertaining and instructive imaginary dialogue between Kautilya and his near-contemporary Plato see S. Ookerjee, *Plato and the Arthasastra* (Mumbai, 2010).

273 The Bodh-Gaya sculptures, A. M. Coomaraswamy, *Ars Asiatica* 18 (1935); roundels, PLS. 51.3; 52.2,4; the folded dress, PL. 39. Winged elephant, London, V&A.

274 J.E. van Lohuizen-de Leeuw in *Aspects of Indian Art* (ed. P. Pal, 1972) 28–43. J.P. Vogel, *La Sculpture de Mathura: Ars Asiatica* 15 (1930). M.L. Carter, *Bull.Cleveland Mus.* Oct. 1982, 246–57 on the 'Dionysiac' behaviour on the pillar in Cleveland (Czuma 1985 no. 42), and on Dionysiac aspects of Kushan art in *Ars Orientalis* 7 (1968) 121–46.

275 *DCAA* 139, fig. 4.82 (Delhi NM 2800). It is a moot point whether the woman is drunk, or simply kneeling/fleeing; see D.M. Stadtner in *Orientations* Jan. 1996, 39–46, where later groups with the harlot Vasantasena are adduced and associated with a myth and early Indian play.

276 Athenaeus 10.437a,b.

277 On Greeks, wine and India, K. Karttunen, *India in early Greek Literature* (Helsinki, 1989) 207–10. And cf. J. Boardman, *The Triumph of Dionysos* (Oxford BAR, 2014).

278 Karttunen, op. cit., 212–8.

279 Mathura Museum. Photo, C. Kontoleon.

280 Boston, from Mathura: *Marg* 39.4 (1988) 17, fig. 17. *Ars Asiatica* 15 (1930) PL. 5.5.

281 C. Wolff, *Rev.Et.Anc.* 101 (1999) 390.

282 W. Vogelsang, *SAS* 4 (1988) 103–13. Achaemenid Persian rule may not have extended much beyond Taxila: D. Fleming, *BAI* 9 (1993) 67–72.

283 On Taxila: the three-volume publication by its excavator, Sir John Marshall, *Taxila* (Cambridge, 1951) and his detailed *Guide to Taxila* (ed.4, 1960); Rahman Dar, *Taxila*, and in *Urban Form and Meaning in South Asia* (eds H. Spodek, D.M. Srinavasan, Washington Studies 31, 1993) 103–22; F.R. Allchin, *The Archaeology of Early Historic South Asia* (Cambridge, 1995) *passim*.

284 R. Stoneman, *JHS* 115 (1995) 99–114.

285 Useful essays on Kharoshti scripts in *Akademie Aktuell* 2013.1, 4–57.

286 *Taxila* PLS. 73a, 120a.

287 Cf. Colledge, 126, 134. Rahman Dar 1984 argues for its Greekness and early date. Bernard doubts Philostratos' reliability for information about Taxila: *Topoi* 6.2 (1996) 504–30.

288 G.E. Medleycott, *India and the Apostle Thomas* (1905); J.N. Farquhar, 'The Apostle Thomas in North India', *Bull.J.Rylands Library* 10 (1926) 80ff. and 11 (1927) 20ff. The columns were perhaps at Kasur. The altars, Pliny, *Nat.Hist.* 6.62.

289 R.E.M. Wheeler, *Charsada* (Oxford, 1962) PL. 40.A2 – the sealing; *DCAA* 135, fig. 4.76 (a Herakles). For more recent views on the site and its dating see Mairs 2011, 37.

290 Maues as a Saka king of an Indo-Greek kingdom, F. Widemann, *East and West* 53 (2003) 95–115.

291 Galli 2011, 299, fig. 6, a relief from Butkara in Rome.

292 H.P. Francfort, *Ars asiatiques* 32 (1976) 91–8.

293 On dating, C. Lo Muzio, *ACSS* 17 (2011) 331–40.

294 *Les Palettes de Gandhara* (MDAF 23, 1979). Important remarks and additions in *Lotus*, and see J. Pons' essay and illustrations in *Gandhara* 153–175 – on *ketos*, Herakles and Dionysos motifs. Francfort listed 97 examples. Rahman Dar 150 examples (1984, 99–142). Other sources include: P. Pal, *Indian Sculpture* 1 (Los Angeles, 1986) S31a-c; Czuma, 1985, 150–3; Galli 2011, 296–302; C. Louzio, *ACSS* 17 (2011) 331–40, chronology (most, 1st/2nd centuries AD). See also now http://claude.rapin.free.fr/5Gandhara7%20images_fichiers/5GandharaCLR7.htm for a largely 'new' private collection of 17 pieces.

295 Francfort, no. 6; *Crossroads* no. 154.

296 Francfort, no. 14; *Gandhara* 166, fig. 24; an apparently abbreviated version, ibid., 167, fig. 25.

297 J. Boardman, *The World of Ancient Art* (2006) PL. 142.

298 *Lotus* no. 17.

299 Francfort, no. 1; also *Lotus* no. 18.

300 Francfort, no. 3, and compare the erotic nos. 4, 10, 11, 18.

301 Francfort, no. 15.

302 *Gandhara* no. 21; and Paris, Guimet Museum.

303 *Lotus* no. 26; Czuma 1985, no. 71.

304 Francfort, no. 8; *Crossroads* no. 153.

305 Galli 2011, 297, fig. 4c.

306 Francfort, no. 2. He pulls at the dress of a woman on a clay relief vase in Lahore Museum, *LIMC* IV, Herakles no. 1546.

307 *Lotus* no. 24; *Gandhara* 168, fig. 27, and probably a drunken Herakles again on fig. 28, and Francfort, no. 13.

308 *DCAA* 117, fig. 4.51.

309 Francfort, no. 17.

310 Francfort, no. 49; the female version, Rahman Dar 1984,, no. 133 (in Tokyo).

311 Ancient Orient Museum.

312 *Lotus* no. 19.

313 Francfort, no. 16.

314 Francfort, no. 1.

315 *L'Or des Amazones* (ed. V. Schiltz, Musée Cernuschi, 2001) nos. 216 ff. And the dish in a Sarmatian context, *Antiquity* 37 (1963) PL. 23.

316 Francfort, nos. 41 (replica, Czuma 1985, no. 70), 42; cruder, nos. 43, 44.

317 Los Angeles Museum of Art 2003.70; accompanied by an Eros.

318 Rapin, op. cit., no. 1, and compare the harpist, Francfort, no. 7.

319 *Gandhara* 156, fig. 1.

320 Francfort, no. 9.

321 And without the Eros, *Gandhara* 156, fig. 3; a winged Greek female, and a naked boy as rider, ibid., 158, figs. 8, 9. Cf. Francfort, no. 53; Christies, NY Sale 1640, lot 12.

322 Francfort, no. 12; Berlin, Ind.Mus.: M. Hallade, *The Gandhara Style* (1968) 25, PL. 19.

323 Internet photo.

324 Francfort, no. 24. With a ram's head and ridden by a boy, Francfort, no. 23. Lion's head and boy riders, Francfort, nos. 33–36.

325 Internet photo.

326 *Lotus* no. 22. On the possible local heroic character of the 'Nereid' figures, M.L. Carter, *BAI* 6 (1992) 67–78.

327 Rapin, op. cit., no. 5.

328 *BAI* 10 (1996) 273. Private.

329 *BAI* 10 (1996) 272–3; they are male, wearing tunics. Oxford EA 1996.82. A youth riding a hippocamp appears on one found in far-off Tajikistan (*Oxus* no. 45)

330 *Lotus* no. 21, with Eros.

331 Francfort, PLS. 28–32. On Parthian belt plaques see V.S. Curtis, *Iranica Antiqua* 36 (2001) 299–328.

332 Oxford EA 1977.22, 204. Cf. *Crossroads* no. 142, and O.M. Dalton, *The Treasure of the Oxus* (London, 1964) nos. 199, 200, with elephants. On her see E. Knauer, *Coats, Queens and Cormorants* (2009)

'The Queen Mother of the West' 435–67, fig. 47 (= pp. 62–115 in V.H. Mair (ed.), *Contact and Exchange* (Hawaii, 2006) fig. 45). Later, cf. the clay roundel from Afrasiab, L. Albaum and B. Brentjes, *Wächter des Goldes* (1972) PL. 107.

333 *GGFR* 320–2. On Greco-Persian in Bactria see E.E. Kuz'mina, *Colloques CNRS* 567, 201–14.

334 *GGFR* PLS. 965, 974.

335 *GGFR* PL. 986.

336 *GGFR* 320–1, fig. 309; properly explained in Sherwin-White/Kuhrt 1993, 32.

337 *Lotus* no. 16.

338 In Kuwait. Publication by S. Middleton forthcoming.

339 G. Fussmann, *Rev.Num.* 6 (1972) PL. 1.1.

340 *GGFR* 318–8, the Taxila Group, figs. 303–5; the Alexander [PL. VIII], ibid., PL. 998 (also Boardman/Vollenweider, *Oxford* I, no. 280). *DCAA* 118–9. Peshawar Museum houses several examples in the Greco-Persian tradition, including scaraboids. For a lapidary hoard at Taxila, M. Treister and S. Yatsenko, *SRAA* 5 (1998) 74–5. For classicizing gems from NW India see also *Cambridge History of India* I (1922) 647, PL. 33; J. Marshall, *Taxila* 2 (1951) ch. 31.

341 *TT* figs. 69–73, 74 (Greco-Persian), 108. *CII* no. 89bis.

342 *DCAA* 79, fig. 4.5 (Missouri Univ.). Another, M. Henig, *The Content Cameos* (1990) no. 141.

343 British Museum.

344 London, V&A 14.1948.408A.

345 A. Sen-Gupta, *East and West* 54 (2004) 65–7, fig. 1.

346 P. Callieri, *Seals and Sealings from the north-west of the Indian Subcontinent and Afghanistan* (4th century BC–11th century AD (Naples, 1997); 'Seals from Gandhara' in *BCH* Suppl. 29 (1996) 413–22. The finds of seals and sealings go far back to early days of exploration; cf. A. Stein, in *Geographical Journal* July/Sept. 1909, 20, in *On Ancient Central Asian Tracks* (1932), 89, 104, in *Prel. Rept. Chinese Turkestan* (1901) PLS. 9 (sealings), 13, in *Ancient Khotan* (1907) PLS. 71–2 (sealings), in *Innermost Asia* (1928) PLS. 10, 111; B. Brentjes in *Baghd.Mitt.* 20 (1989) 315–35; *Camb.Hist.India* I (1922) 647–8, PL. 33; E.E. Kuzmina, *Le Plateau Iranien* (1977) 201ff.; *Taxila* PLS. 197–8, 207–8. It is still debatable whether there is any western influence on the shapes of some pre-Han seals in China.

347 *Crossroads* nos. 151–2.

348 J.C. Harle, in *South Asian Archaeology 1983; Ist.Univ. Or.Napoli, Series Minor* XXIII (1985), 641–52. The group recurs in a more Indian style on a stone

weight (New York, Met.Mus.) and elsewhere where it clearly signifies Krishna and the horse-demon Kesin, including the apparent thrusting of an arm in its mouth which is no more than suggested by Greek scenes.

349 *A Golden Treasury* (V&A, 1988) nos. 11, 12, 14.

350 F. Widemann in T. Hacken (ed.), *Technology and analysis of ancient gemstones* (*PACT* 23, 1987) 175, fig. 1; inscribed 'of Shaura'.

351 Cf. A.D.H. Bivar, *Numismatic Society of India Golden Jubilee issue* 23 (1961) 309–27.

352 P. Bernard, O. Bopearachchi, 'Deux bracelets grecs', *Journal des Savants* 2002, 237–78. *CII* nos. 154–5.

353 *DCAA* 87, fig. 4.19. B. Litvinsky, *JIAAA* 1 (2006) 85–8. On Eros earrings, P. Calmeyer, *Fest. Van den Berghe* 605ff.

354 *Crossroads* no. 140; *DCAA* 118; *CII* no. 156; Boardman in *GAC* 11–15, comparing a gold earring from the Punjab in Berlin (fig. 7); a similar one from near Dushanbe, *Oxus* no. 23; and Shirley Day Ltd. (91B Jermyn St.), *East of the Oxus* (1995) no. 6. Classical figure types on earrings in the east: B. Mussche, *Vorderasiatischer Schmuck* (1988) 65–8, pl II; C. Fabrègues, *JIAAA* 1 (2006) 71–87 – and Persian.

355 *Jewellery Studies* 5 (1991) 91–2. *IAW* PL. 9 (K. Fischer). For jewels of this type in the Sarmatian world see M. Treister in *Iranica Antiqua* 39 (2004) 297–321.

356 *DCAA* 118, fig. 4.52 (Taxila); 146, fig. 4.92; *TTG* figs. 13, 14.

357 *Crossroads* no. 138; cf. no. 137 for the dressed goddess with a mirror, from Taxila.

358 *Crossroads* no. 159.

359 *Crossroads* no. 97; Galli 2011, 305–6. On Hellenistic silver in the east, M. Carter, *BAI* 9 (1995) 257–66; M. Pfrommer, *Metalwork from the Hellenized East* (Malibu, 1993).

360 *Crossroads* no. 99.

361 For the rest of the hoard and inscriptions, F. Baratte, *Journal des Savants* 2001, 249–319. Cups from Gandhara inscribed in both Greek and Kharoshti, *CII* nos. 88bis,ter.

362 *Crossroads* no. 101; London, BM OA 1937.3–19.1.

363 J.-C. Gardin in *Aus dem Osten des Alexander-reiches* (Fest. K. Fischer, 1984) 110–26.

364 Idem, *Berlin Kongress 1988* , 187–97; *Litvinsky Festschrift* 423; in *de l'Indus aux Balkans* (Recueil J. Deshayes; ed. J.-C. Huot, 1985) 447–60. On the dating of Hellenistic pottery in Central Asia, B. Lyonnet, *ACSS* 18 (1912) 143–77.

365 For the full publication see J. Hackin et al., *Recherches arch. à Begram* (1939); *Nouvelles rech. à Begram* (1954). S. Mehendale, *Cahiers d'Asie Centrale* 1/2 (1996) 47–64.

366 D. Whitehouse, *J. Roman Archaeology* 2 (1989) 93–100.

367 *DCAA* 123, fig. 4.60. A case has been made for dating the ivories earlier, 1st-century BC, but there is nothing else at Begram really to support this: J.L. Davidson, in *Aspects of Indian Art* (ed. P. Pal, 1972) 1–14. He also notes the rinceaux which he traces to Bharhut and Sanchi rather than the west (pp. 8–9) but they also had a long Greek history. For a relatively early date, L. Nehru in *SRAA* 10 (2004) 97–150.

368 *DCAA* 123, fig. 4.61.

369 *Afghanistan* (NY) nos. 147–9.

370 Cf. *DCAA* 120, fig. 4.58; M. Menninger, *Würzburger Forschungen zur Altertumskunde* 1 (1996); *Untersuchungen zu den Gläsen und Gipsabgüssen...Begram*). D. Whitehouse, *AJA* 102 (1998) 639–41.

371 *DCAA* 120, fig. 4.57.

372 *Dossiers d'Archéologie* 341 (2010) 43, at Khalchayan, with Greek Victories overhead.

373 Ball 2000 gives an excellent, detailed and well illustrated conspectus of Roman influence and construction especially in the near-Near East. Also, on the historical perspective, F. Millar, *The Roman Near East* (Cambridge, 1993); and *Eastern Frontiers of the Roman Empire* (eds D. French, C. Lightfoot, Oxford BAR 553, 1989).

374 On the survival of Hellenistic styles see M. Waelkens in S. Walker and A. Cameron (eds) *The Greek Renaissance in the Roman Empire* (London, ICS Bull. Supl. 55, 1989) 77–88. On Roman emperors visiting the east, A. Horstein and S. Lalance (eds), *Les voyages des Empereurs dans l'Orient Romain* (Arles, 2012).

375 J. Freely, *Children of Achilles. The Greeks in Asia Minor* (London, 2010) gives a useful account.

376 V. Dehija, 'India's Visual Narratives' in G.H.R. Tillotson (ed.), *Paradigms of Indian Architecture* (Richmond, 1998) 80–106.

377 Best on the Roman effects is H. Buchthal's good essay, 'The Western aspects of Gandharan Sculpture', *Proc.Brit.Acad.* 21 (1945), 151–76. And see A.C. Soper, 'The Roman Style in Gandhara', *AJA* 55 (1951) 301–19. B. Rowland, 'Gandhara, Rome and Mathura; The Early Relief Style', *Archives of the Chinese Art Society of America* 10 (1956) 8–17. M. Wheeler, *Rome beyond the Imperial*

Frontiers (Penguin, 1955) Part Three; he subsumes Asian Greeks with Romans for this period, so has 'Romano-Buddhist art'. His excavating style has come under some criticism, as by W.A. Fairservis in *Iosephi Tucci Mem. Dedicata* (1987) 343–54. Ball 2000, 139–48 ('no journeymen craftsmen'). A good and well-illustrated general account – S.L. Huntington, *The Art of Ancient India* (1985). H.C. Ackermann, *Narrative Stone Reliefs from Gandhara in the V&A* (Rome, 1975) also studies the 'Roman' effects and suggests that illustrated book scrolls might have been a source.

378 E.g., those from Nihavand: R. Ghirshman, *CRAI* 1948, 335; *Parthes et Sassanides* (1962) 18, fig. 23.

379 On the coinage, Rahman Dar 1984, ch. 6. Some hundred Roman coins have been found in Kushan India. To suggest that thousands of others must have been melted down seems desperate.

380 H. Dodge in *Architecture and architectural sculpture in the Roman Empire* (ed. M. Henig, 1990) 108–20.

381 Cf. L. Casson, *The Periplus Maris Erythraei* (1989); *DCAA* 332, n. 138; Xinru Liu, *The Silk Road in World History* (Oxford, 2010), 34–41. *Rome and India. The Ancient Sea Trade* (eds V. Begley, R de Puma, Univ. Wisconsin, 1991). J.-F. Salles, *Topoi* 3 (1993) 493–510. The Yemen en route had its share of trade, as in classical bronzes, cf. R. Fleischer and R. Schulz, *Arch.Ber.aus dem Yemen* 13 (2012) 1–90.

382 Pliny, *Nat.Hist.* 6.101. F. Warmington, *The Commerce between the Roman Empire and India* (1928). P. Turner, *Roman Coins from India* (1989). J. Puskas in *IAW* 141–56 on trade contacts. For Ceylon, there were imports from as early as the Hellenistic period – seals (see above), and pottery: J. Bouzek, *Berlin Kongress 1988*, 316–7. On external contacts in Ceylon, *Archiv Orientalni* 61 (1993) 13–28. A Rhodian architect Amphilochos seems to have gained a reputation for working in India (Warmington, 61–2). A good short account of Rome and south India in R.E.M. Wheeler, *Rome beyond the Imperial Frontiers* (1954) ch. 12. Essays in *Rome and India* (eds V. Begley, P. de Puma, 1991), on routes and trade. http://oxrep.classics.ox.ac.uk/bibliographies/ has a good bibliography on Indo-Roman trade.

383 H. Harrauer and P.J. Sijpesteijn, *Anz.Österr.Akad. Wiss.* 122 (1985) 124–55. Dio Chrysostom, *Disc.* 32, 40 'I behold among you not only Greeks and Italians and peoples from neighbouring Syria,

Libya, Cilicia, not merely Ethiopians and Arabs from more distant regions, but even Bactrians and Scythians and Persians and a few Indians'.

384 Harle 1986, 82, fig. 62.

385 B.N. Mukherjee, *Marg* 38 (1986) 81–2. H. P. Ray, *Topoi* 3 (1993) 455–80. Indo-Greek Buddhists, J.D. Lerner, *AJA* 102 (1998) 393.

386 Envoys from Bactria to Hadrian and Antoninus: A.C. Soper, *AJA* 55 (1951) 305. D.F. Graf, 'The Roman East from the Chinese perspective', *Les Annales Arch. Arabes Syriennes* 42 (1996) 1–18.

387 *Crossroads* no. 197. The obverse shows Kanishka I in the traditional Asian frontal pose: *DCAA* 124, fig. 4.62. On use of Greek script, Mairs 2011, 43.

388 S.M. Burstein, *AWE* 9 (2010) 181–92.

389 N. Sims-Williams and J. Cribb, *SRAA* 4 (1995/6) 75–142.

390 On which J.D.M Derrett, *J. of the Royal Asiatic Soc.* 2 (1992) 47–57.

391 Ball 2000, 139–48.

392 Basic sources are: Nehru, *OGS*. Czuma 1985. J. Marshall, *The Buddhist Art of Gandhara* (1960). E. Errington, *SAA* 1987, 765–81. *Gandharan Art in Context* (eds R. Allchin et al., New Delhi, 1997). K. Walton Dobbins gives an illustrated account of Gandharan art from stratified excavations (correlated with coins) in *East and West* 23 (1973) 279–94. Also for coin dating, E. Errington in *SRAA* 6 (1999/2000). Bibliography 1950–93, P. Guenée, *Bibl. Analytique* (Paris, 1998). On the question of 'Orientalised Hellenism' or the 'Hellenised Orient', A. Filigenzi, *ACSS* 18 (2012) 111–41.

393 A.D.H. Bivar, 'The Historical Origins of the Art of Gandhara' in *Pakistan Archaeology* 26 (1991) 61–72. On Parthian associations of the dynastic styles, in some detail, K. Weidemann, *JRGZM* 18 (1971) 146–78.

394 Nehru, *OGS* PLS. 39–43, 46–7; *SRAA* 6 (1999/2000) 217–39; G. Frumkin, *Archaeology in Soviet Central Asia* (1970) 114ff.

395 Notably in essays by Facenna et al. in *ACSS* 9 (2003) 277–380.

396 *ACSS* 9 (2003) 373, fig. 54. D. Faccenna, *Butkara* I.2 (1962) PL. 289–90, no. 3215.

397 J. Boardman in *GAC* 3, fig. 1 (London); cf. 5, fig. 2 (Peshawar), 6, fig. 3. *Crossroads* no. 131, cf. no. 130.

398 *Ars Asiatica* 15 (1930) PL. 34b. Cf. Huntington (n. 377) 84, fig. 5.34; 87, fig. 5.38, 119, fig. 7.10

399 See especially M.L. Carter, 'Dionysiac aspects of Kushan art', *Ars Orientalis* 7 (1968) 121–46. Galli

2011, 302–21. Also, with the theatrical aspects in view, P. Brancaccio and Xinru Liu in *Journal of Global History* 4 (2009)227–44.

400 *DCAA* 127, fig. 4.66 (Paris, Guimet Museum, from Hadda).

401 J. Boardman, *The Archaeology of Nostalgia* (2002) 124, fig. 92; *The Triumph of Dionysos* (Oxford BAR, 2014).

402 Carter, op. cit., 121–3, fig. 1; fig. 5 for a wine-making scene not Greek in inspiration.

403 Ibid., fig. 6.

404 *Bull. Cleveland Museum of Art* Oct. 1982, 254, fig. 14. Lahore Museum 1914.

405 *DCAA* 127, fig. 4.65 (London); and the bronze monster, ibid., 141, fig. 4.85, much later.

406 *DCAA* 130, fig. 4.68 (London). *Crossroads* no. 132. A useful view of Roman sarcophagi of the eastern world in G. Koch, *Sarkophage des römischen Kaiserzeit* (Darmstadt, 1993) chs. 5, 8, 9. And more fully, G. Koch and H. Sichtermann, *Römische Sarkophage* (Munich, 1982) Part V.

407 *DCAA* 132–3, figs. 4.71 (London), 4.72a (Boston).

408 *Crossroads* no. 193.

409 *DCAA* 130, fig. 4.68. And *Taxila* PL. 216.72–3. C.A. Bromberg, *BAI* 2 (1988) 67–85 on the putti with garlands in Asia. Several at Jamalgarhi, Errington, PL. 87.

410 *DCAA* 136, fig. 4.78 (London). *Crossroads* no. 133.

411 N.A. Khan, in *East and West* 40 (1990) 315–9.

412 *Crossroads* no. 128 (London). Cf. Carter, fig. 7, a pair of drinking hippo-centaurs, the female winged. A good selection with various animal heads at Andandheri, A.H. Dani, *Ancient Pakistan* 4 (1968–9), PLS. 21–3.

413 *Crossroads* no. 134 (London).

414 Dr Sen-Gupta kindly told me about this. It is from the same complex as reliefs published by M. Taddei in *Marakanda* (Essays... James Harle, 1990). On his further appearances north and east see J.-U. Hartmann in *Jb.Bayerische Akad. der Wiss.* 2004, 107–29.

415 F.B. Flood, 'Herakles and the 'Perpetual Acolyte' of the Buddha' in *SAS* 5 (1989) 17–27.

416 *Aus dem Osten des Alexanderreiches* (Fest. K. Fischer, eds J. Ozols, V. Thewalt, 1984) 159, fig. 9; Stanco, 24.

417 A.D.H. Bivar, 'Cosmopolitan Allusions in the Art of Gandhara' in *Actes, Colloque, Strasbourg 17-18 Mars 2000* (eds Z. Tarzi, D. Vaillancourt, 2005) 15–18.

418 M. Taddei, *East and West* 14 (1963) 38–55. The motif with a trophy appears on the *Gemma Augustea*.

419 *DCAA* 131, fig. 4.69 (London).

420 *ACSS* 3 (1996) 293, fig. 1 (B.Ya. Stavisky; also in *East and West* 23 (1973) 265–77, on capitals in Bactria, and *GAC* 49–50). There is a reclining satyr with a drinking horn and a wreathed hydria on a capital fragment on the Swiss market (1995). Cf. *Berlin Kongress 1988* 63, fig. 1, capital with lion foreparts. From Ananderi, *Ancient Pakistan* 4 (1968–9) PL. 23c, a man's bust. The idea probably comes from the west, e.g., Parthia,. a capital from Warka, J. Curtis (ed.), *Mesopotamia and Iran...* (London, 2000) 29, PL. 6, stucco capital with male bust; or even Greek as at Aphrodisias: K.T. Erim, *Aphrodisias de Carie* (Lille Coll. III, 1987) 31, fig. 23; *idem, Aphrodisias* (London, 1986) 61; and in Colchis, *DCAA* 221, fig. 6.50.

421 *ACSS* 9 (2003) 290, fig. 7; 292, fig. 8. With a Bodhisattva from Jamalgarhi, Majumbar (Errington) II, PL. 13b. On Bactrian capitals, J. Staviskij, *East and West* 23 (1978) 265–77.

422 Sotheby, London, 7 July 1986, nos. 160–2.

423 *DCAA* 132–3, fig. 4.72a,b.

424 *DCAA* 125, fig. 4.63 (once Mardan) – rather 'improved' with boot polish in an English officers' mess.

425 G. Ortiz, *The Ortiz Collection* (London 1994) no. 173; O. Bopearachchi, in *On the Cusp of an Era* (ed. D.M. Srinavasan (2007) 119–32.

426 New York 1986.2, with garnet inlay.

427 M.L. Carter, *Marg* 39.4 (1988), 22

428 *Crossroads* no. 135 (London). *DCAA* 134, fig. 4.73. Further on hair styles, J.C. Harle in *Orientalia Iosephi Tucci Mem. Dicata: Serie Orientale Roma* LVI.2 (1987) 569–72.

429 *Crossroads* no. 136 (London). *DCAA* 134, fig. 4.74; cf. fig. 4.75 for a more complete rendering of a Greek Tyche.

430 Classical types of children in Gandharan art: A. Provenzali, *Parthica* 7 (2005) 155–76; the Greek gesture of hand to chin, K.Tanabe, *Parthica* 12 (2010) 81–94.

431 Thus, *DCAA* 140, figs. 4.83–4, the ever popular Herakles and Tyche/Fortuna.

432 *Crossroads* nos. 102–5 (Herakles), no. 107 (Eros), no. 108 (Dionysos or a symposiast), no. 110 (Demeter), no. 111 (Tyche), and compare the Indian and classicized versions of a naked woman, nos. 113–4.

433 New York: A. Herakles. B. wrestlers, one lifting the other, a common Greek motif: Galli 2011, 293, fig. 1a,b. Czuma 1985, no. 81 (Krishna and horse).

434 *DCAA* 142, figs. 4.87–8. On the Hadda
sculptures, M.Z. Tarzi, *CRAI* 1976, 381–410.
P. Cambon, *MonPiot* 83 (2004) 131–84 for Hadda
sculpture in the Musée Guimet, including
a splendidly classical male nude, 152, fig. 44,
and a very classical, dressed figure, 158, fig. 55.
C. Mustamandy in *Fest. K. Fischer* (1984) 176–80
(and for other Hadda sculpture).

435 *DCAA* 138, fig. 4.81 (Calcutta).

436 *DCAA* 135, fig. 4.77 (Karachi).

437 *DCAA* 138, fig. 4.79 (London, from Jamalgarhi).
Pictures of Atlas figures in Ingholt, figs. 381–6.

438 *Crossroads* no. 126 (London); q.v. for centaurs.
Statuettes: Czuma 1985, nos. 97 (winged), 98.

439 E.g., the famous bronze rhyton from the
Northwest Frontier [PL. XXX]. One carries an
Indian rider on Sanchi stupa 2, and they appear
holding flowers and bowls on stone reliefs at
Lucknow, from Mathura. They survive even
into Sasanian art – a splendid centauress with
flowers on a gilt silver dish: *Schätze des Orients*
(Meisterwerke...Miho Museum, Vienna, 1999)
no. 49.

440 The device beside him is unexplained.

441 *DCAA* 138, fig. 4.81.

442 P. Brancaccio and Xinru Liu, 'Dionysus and
drama in the Buddhist art of Gandhara', *Journal
of Global History* 4 (2009) 219–244, esp. 239–44.
Dionysos in India, A. Dihle, in *India and the
Ancient World* (ed. G. Pollet, 1987) 47–58.

Chapter 7

443 *DCAA* 81, figs. 4.7,8.

444 *Defence of the Roman Byzantine East* (eds
D. Freeman, P. Kennedy; Oxford BAR 279, 1986).

445 See Colledge ch.7 for a good account of Parthian
architecture. And in general, J. Wiesehöfer (ed.)
Das Partherreich und seine Zeugnisse (1998). On
Roman arts in Parthia, the *interpretatio romana*,
M. Colledge, in M. Henig and A. King (eds)
Pagan Gods (Oxford 1986) 221–30. *From Persepolis
to the Punjab* (eds E. Errington, V.S. Curtis,
British Museum, 2007) for valuable essays on
the period. Herrmann 1977 for arts and sites.

446 A.M. Smith, *Roman Palmyra* (Oxford, 2013).

447 *After Alexander* 24, fig. 16; British Museum.

448 *DCAA* 84, fig. 4.13 (Teheran Museum); *Persica* 16
(2000) 33.

449 *DCAA* 84, fig. 4.12 (Teheran Museum); *Cambridge
Hist.Iran* 3.2, PL. 65. *CII* no. 3.

450 *CII* nos. 18–27; ibid., nos. 73–4 for slightly later
parchment records from Media recording sales

of vineyards, in Greek, and no. 75, a 'Herakles
lives here; let no evil enter' on a base.

451 Herrmann 1977, 55, below; Baghdad Museum.

452 A. Invernizzi, *Parthica* 1 (1999) 107–17 (a dying
Amazon figure); R. Menegazzi, *Parthica* 7 (2005)
81–91, figures of women.

453 *DCAA* 85–6, fig. 4.15. Herrmann 1977, 67–72.
E. J. Keall, M.A. Leveque and N. Willson, *Iran* 18
(1980) 1–41.

454 Colledge, PL. 64. On such figures, J.-M. Dentzer
in *Annales arch. arabes syriennes* 21 (1971) 39–50.
On Allat/Athena see J. Starcky in *Mythologies
Périphériques* (eds, L. Kahil, C Augé, Paris, 1981)
119–130; ibid., 107–12, A. Bounni on Apollo at
Palmyra.

455 Colledge, 157–9 and in *Pagan Gods* (see n. 135)
224, fig. 2 [fig. 136]; 227, fig, 6 [fig. 135, Allat].
Cf. S. Downey, *AJA* 72 (1968) 211–7. For Herakles
figures at Hatra and Palmyra and their
relationship to Nergal see T. Kaizer, *Iraq* 62
(2000) 219–32.

456 Los Angeles M.76.97.592. For the pairs,
Crossroads no. 145; A. Post, *Boreas* 18 (1995)
247–54.

457 Latest work on the archaeology of Sasanian
Persia: *Persia's Imperial Power in Late Antiquity*
(eds E.W. Sauer et al., 2013). A good overview,
but not for art, is T. Daryaee, *Sasanian Persia*
(London, 2009). On the conflict with Rome,
P.M. Edwell, *Between Rome and Persia* (2008)
ch. 5. On classical elements in Sasanian art,
E. Will, *BCH Suppl.* XIV (1985), 433–45.

458 For the rock reliefs see Herrmann 1977, 87–94.
The Emperor Gordian may also be trampled by
the Sasanian king. The cameo – H. von Gall,
Das Reiterkampfbild (1990) 56–9. Paris, Cabinet
des Medailles (Babelon no. 360).

459 On the techniques, W.T. Chase, *Ars Orientalia* 7
(1968) 75ff.; shapes, R. Ghirshman, *Ars Orientalis* 2
(1957) 77–82, and ibid., 56–7, 68,

460 *Afghanistan* no. 179; Lukonin, fig. 216;
P. Denwood, *Iran* 11 (1973) 121–6. A cup in
Cleveland (66.369) carries a scroll containing
wingless erotes-musicians.

461 The silver cups, here figs. 139–43 are *DCAA* 90–
96, figs. 4.23–6. K. Weitzmann, *The Art Bulletin* 25
(1943) 289–324 on the Euripidean aspect. A good
discussion in A.C. Gunter and P. Jett, *Ancient
Iranian Metalwork in the Arthur M. Sackler Gallery*
(1992) 148–54. On 'Kushano-Sasanian bowls'
P. Harper in *Misc. Van den Berghe* (1989) 847–66,
and cf. 915, PL. 2b.

462 The technique is well described by Jett, ibid., 49–60.

463 P.O. Harper, *Mesopotamia* 22 (1987) 341–55.

464 I discuss these in *DCAA* 94–7, figs. 4.27–9; *Classical Art in Eastern Translation* (17th J.L. Myres Memorial Lecture; Oxford, Leopard Press, 1993); and *The Triumph of Dionysos* (Oxford, 2014) 22–4). Also now, M. Compareti in *Parthica* 9 (2007) 216–9.

465 A.S. Melikian-Chirvani, 'Rustam and Herakles, a Family Resemblance' in *BAI* 12 (1998) 171–99.

466 The figures are taken for Dionysos and Ariadne in Gunter and Kett, op. cit., 121, and the satyr/countryman for Herakles. Ettinghausen, *BSI* 4, also takes the main figure for male; it is certainly more fully dressed than most Sasanian women.

467 Observed too by M.M. Kouhpar and T. Taylor, in *Current Res. in Sas. Archaeology* (Oxford, BAR 2008) 127–135. P. Callieri, ibid., 115–126, on Dionysiac themes in Sasanian architecture.

468 G. Ortiz, *The Ortiz Collection* (1994) no. 243.

469 British Museum. And cf. (wingless) on the cup, Dalton, no. 208, PL. 38, and p. 64 where the 'genie' is discussed.

470 Lukonin, fig. 146.

471 *Schätze des Orients* (Meisterwerke. Miho Museum, Vienna, 1999) no. 45.

472 Lukonin II, fig. 37 (Hermitage).

473 Lukonin II, fig. 195 (Hermitage).

474 B. Brentjes in J. Davis-Kimball et al. (eds), *Kurgans, Ritual Sites and Settlements. Eurasian Bronze and Iron Age* (Oxford BAR Int. series 890, 2000) 259–68. A.D.H. Bivar, *Art et archéologie des monastères gréco-buddhistes* (Colloq. int. du Crpoga, 2000, eds Tarzi and Vaillancourt) 10–23; and in *Pakistan Archaeology* 26.1 (1991) 68–9.

475 They appear on another dish, heads lowered, without their attendants: Ettinghausen, *BSI*, fig. 40; idem., ch.2, thinks the winged-horse motif is of some importance in Sasanian art.

476 Ettinghausen, *BSI*, figs. 49–57.

477 Thus, Ettinghausen, *BSI*, ch. 1. On festal scenes in Sasanian art, M.L. Carter, *Acta Iranica* 1 (1974) 171–202.

478 G. Azarpay, *Iranica Antiqua* 23.1 (1988) 349–60, also for the Dioskouroi.

479 *CRAI* 2007, 563, fig. 17; Cabinet des Medailles, Paris, 1975.251.12.

480 At Taq-I Bustan.

481 Corduba – in the V&A. Faras, British Museum.

482 See J. Boardman in *Festschrift Vincent Megaw* (2015), and *AWE* (forthcoming).

Epilogue

483 J. Boardman, *RA* 1972, 57–72.

484 J. Boardman, *The Archaeology of Nostalgia* (London, 2002), 160–2.

485 E. Benjamin, *Classical Quarterly* 51 (2001) 115–26. On Greek views on Amazons and nomad women, T. David, *Artibus Asiae* 32 (1970) 203–25; and *Ars Asiatiques* 32 (1976) 203–25.; J. Davis-Kimball, *SRAA* 5 (1998) 1–50.

486 J. Boardman, *The Archaeology of Nostalgia* (London, 2002), 127–32.

487 *Ibid.*, 106–7.

488 Strabo 688. In general on Greek sources about Herakles and Dionysos in India see P.A. Brunt in the Loeb *Arrian* II, 435–42.

489 A. Furtwängler-K. Reichhold, *Griechische Vasenmalerei* (Munich, 1904–32) PL. 72.3. In general on Dionysos and the east see J. Boardman, *The Triumph of Dionysos* (Oxford BAR, 2014).

490 For the iconography of Astarte, much studied, see L.A. Cakmak in *Gandhara* 76–9. Z. Bahrani writes about the hellenization of Ishtar in *Oxford Art Journal* 19.2 (1996) 3–16, but fails to take the point about the utter realism of Greek statuary and its probable effect – remembering of course that it was realistically coloured. Eastern arts were coloured but 'unreal', and were even quick to abandon any of the ideas about real portraiture introduced by Greek coinage, coming to rely on inscriptions, pose, attributes or dress for identification.

491 Ebba Koch, *Shah Jahan and Orpheus* (Graz, 1988), PLS. 15–23.

492 Oxford, Ashmolean Museum EA 1995.3. Cf. I. Weber, *Deutsche, niederlandische... Renaissance Plaketten* (Munich, 1976) no. 698.

Addenda

There are several relevant articles in *Indian Historical Review* 32.1 (2005): Arora on Onesikritos (pp. 35–102); Bopearachchi on new art evidence (pp. 103–25); Davaras on interesting parallels between Bronze Age Greece and early India (pp. 126–39); Gupta on Indo-Roman ocean trade (pp. 140–64); a review article by Holt on studies of Greeks in India (pp. 288–97). The volume is shortly being reissued with some new articles. A. Mayor, *The Amazons* (Princeton, 2014) has much of relevance. L. Nehru, *The Arts of Western Central Asia, 6th century BC to 4th century AD* (Oxford, 2015) will also have much of relevance, especially for the Parthian period. On palettes, H. Falk in *BAI* 24 (2010) 89–113.

Sources of illustrations

Indian Museum, Calcutta/akg-images/Jean-Louis Nou XXXVII; George Ortiz Collection/akg-images XLI; Hermitage Museum, St Petersburg/akg-images I; Alsdorf Collection 89; Museum of Anatolian Civilisations, Ankara IV; Archaeological Museum, Kiev, Ukraine/Photo © Boltin Picture Library/ Bridgeman Images II; Ashmolean Museum, University of Oxford/Bridgeman Images VIII; Bull Collection 88; *Bulletin of the Asia Institute* 71; The Iraq Museum, Baghdad 135, 136, 137; Merz Collection, Bern University 37; J. Boardman 6, 20, 21, 22, 23, 24, 28 (above), 57, 58, 59, 61, 62, 63, 64, 74, 97, 99, 130, 151, VI (bottom left), VI (bottom right), XI, XLII; J. Boardman, *The Relief Plaques of Eastern Eurasia and China*, BAR S2146, Archaeopress, Oxford, 2010 XXVIII; O. Bopearachchi, *Monnaies gréco-bactriennes et indo-grecques, Catalogue raisonné*, Bibliothèque Nationale, Paris 1991 XXIII, XXV; Museum of Fine Arts, Boston 36; Bowdoin College Museum of Art, Brunswick, Maine 9; Indian Museum, Calcutta 68, 69, 70, 125; *China Digest* 66; Museum of Art and Archaeology, University of Missouri, Columbia 96; A. M. Coomaraswamy, *The Bodh-Gaya sculptures*, Ars Asiatica 18, 1935 72; © Reza/Webistan/Corbis 40; Marion Cox 95, 101; P. Denwood, *Iran II*, 1973 142; A. Furtwängler and K. Reichhold, *Griechische Vasenmalere*, Munich, 1904–32 152; G. Gnoli and A. Ivantchik (eds), *Ancient Civilizations from Scythia to Siberia*, Brill 1995 118; Museum für Kunst und Gewerbe, Hamburg IX; E. Heinrich, *Abhandlungen der Preussischen Akademie*, Berlin, 1935 131; F. Holt and O. Bopearachchi (eds), *The Alexander Medallion*, Imago Lattara, 2011 VII; A. Invernizzi, *Parthica 3*, 2001 31, 32, 33, 34, X; Archaeology Museum, Istanbul III; Peter Jackson 2.11; National Museum of Afghanistan, Kabul 49, 103, 104, XVII, XXXI, XXXII, XXXIII, XXXIV, XXXV, XLIII; Nelson-Atkins Museum of Art, Kansas City 86; National Museum of Pakistan, Karachi 126; Anna Kouremenos , Sujatha Chandrasekaran and Roberto Rossi (eds), *From Pella to Gandhara*, BAR Int. Series no. 2221, Archaeopress, Oxford, 2011 XL; W. Kleiss, *Archäologische Mitteilungen aus Iran 3*, Neue Folge, 1970 38; Kreitman Collection, *The Crossroads of Asia*, The Ancient India and Iran Trust, 1992 frontispiece, 1, XXXVI; T. Kruglikova, *Drevnyaya Battriya*, Moscow, 1976 46; Lahore Museum, Pakistan 111; British Museum, London 11, 12, 14, 16, 17, 28 (below), 47, 79, 84, 100, 102, 106, 108, 112, 113, 114, 115, 117, 120, 121, 127, 128, 143, XII; The Trustees of the British Museum, London 2, 39, 132, 146, XLIV; Victoria & Albert Museum, London 85, 97; Los Angeles County Museum of Art. Photo 2014 Scala, Florence 138; J. Paul Getty Museum, Malibu 13; J. Marshall, *Taxila*, Cambridge 1951 76, 77, 78, 105; M. E. Masson and G. A. Pugachenkova, *The Parthian Rhytons of Nisa*, Le Lettere, Florence, 1982 42, 43, 44, 45; Miho Museum, Shigaraki XIII, XIV, XXIX; V. Mordvintseva, *Sarmatische Phaleren*, Rahden, 2001 55, 56; Museo Archaeologico Nazionale, Naples 144; National Museum, New Delhi 73, 80; The Metropolitan Museum of Art, New York, Rogers Fund. 1945 19, Samuel Eilenberg Collection. Gift of Samuel Eilenberg. 1987 82, Samuel Eilenberg Collection. Gift of Samuel Eilenberg. 1987 91, Fletcher Fund. 1963 148, Purchase. 1986 XLII; R. V. Nicholls 3; George Ortiz Collection XLV; Ashmolean Museum, University of Oxford 10, 15, 30, 92, 98, 153, XXX, XXXVIII, XXXIX; *Oxus, 2000 Jahre Kunst am Oxus-Fluss in Mityelasien. Neue Funde aus der Sowjetrepublik Tadschikistan*, Museum Reitburg, Zürich, 1989 41, XVIII, XIX, XX, XXI, XXII; J. Ozols and V. Thewalt, *Aus dem Osten des Alexanderreiches*, Dumont Verlag, Cologne, 1984 116; Bibliothèque Nationale, Paris XXIV; Cabinet des Médailles, Bibliothèque Nationale, Paris 150, XLVI; Musée Guimet, Paris 109; Musée du Louvre, Paris V; Peshawar Museum, Pakistan 83; Private Collection 81, 87, 110; J. Rawson, *Chinese Ornament: The Lotus and the Dragon*, British Museum, London, 1984 65; Museo Nazionale d'Arte Orientale, Rome 107; B. Rowland, *The Art and Architecture of India*, Penguin Books, London, 1977 119; Hermitage Museum, St Petersburg 4, 5, 26, 27, 52, 53, 54, 93, 139, 141, 147; Museum of Fine Arts, Boston. Photo 2014 Scala, Florence 75; The Metropolitan Museum of Art, New York. Photo 2014 Scala, Florence 94, 124; V. Sarianidi, *The Golden Hoard of Bactria*, Aurora Art Publishers, Leningrad, 1985 60; Taisei Corporation ©NHK XV, XVI; M. Z. Tarzi, *Comptes-Rendus de l'Académie des Inscriptions et Belles-Lettres*, 1976 29, 122, 123; Taxila Museum, Pakistan 90; Georgian National Museum, Tbilisi 7; National Museum of Iran, Teheran 25, 133, VI; Museum of Art, Toledo, Ohio 35; Royal Ontario Museum, Toronto 134; UNESCO 129; Urumqi Museum, China 67; Museum of Archaeology, Uşak, Turkey 8; Freer Gallery of Art, Washington D.C. 140, 145, 149.

Acknowledgments

Over the years I have profited from information sent to me by many scholars and from discussion: O. Bopearachchi, A. Sen-Gupta, K. Abdullaev, J. Cribb, E. Errington, P. Stewart, C. Kontoleon, S. Kossak, N. Kreitman, L. Nehru, R.R.R. Smith. I am especially indebted to G.L. Huxley for his comments and corrections. Claudia Wagner has helped me with text and pictures. My daughter Julia has been an invaluable support for travels in Asia since 1989. In Oxford I have enjoyed the continuing hospitality of the Beazley Archive, in the Classical Art Research Centre, Oxford University. The author and publisher also wish to thank collectors and museums recorded in the figure captions and opposite for permission to use illustrations.

General index

Index of places